READING JUNOT DÍAZ

LATINO AND LATIN AMERICAN PROFILES

Frederick Luis Aldama, EDITOR

READING JUNOT DÍAZ

CHRISTOPHER GONZÁLEZ

UNIVERSITY OF PITTSBURGH PRESS

Published by the University of Pittsburgh Press, Pittsburgh, Pa., 15260

Copyright © 2015, University of Pittsburgh Press

Manufactured in the United States of America

Printed on acid-free paper

10 9 8 7 6 5 4 3 2 1

Library of Congress Cataloging-in-Publication Data

González, Christopher.
Reading Junot Díaz / Christopher González.
    pages cm. — (Latino and Latin American Profiles)
Includes bibliographical references and index.
ISBN 978-0-8229-6395-0 (paperback)
1. Díaz, Junot, 1968—Criticism and interpretation. I. Title.
PS3554.I259Z64 2015
813'.54—dc23   2015029545

CONTENTS

ACKNOWLEDGMENTS

The earliest vestiges of this project trace back to a 2007 NPR review by Alan Cheuse of *The Brief Wondrous Life of Oscar Wao* by Junot Díaz. I was so intrigued by the idea of a Latino author who wrote so freely about sci-fi and comics that I had to work extra hard to focus on the road, as I was driving at the time. The novel seemed like a strange brew that was at once so personal and yet so foreign to me. I grew up a Latino kid in the Llano Estacado region of Texas and New Mexico, pretending I was a Jedi in training on Dagobah in my spare time. That was all well and good, but I knew Luke Skywalker wasn't Latino. Additionally, novels by Latinos, which I actively had to seek out since they were conspicuously absent in my secondary school, had never merged the sci-fi and fantasy traditions with the touchstones of my own Latino culture I knew so well, such as the foods, the language, the music, and so forth. After listening to Cheuse's short review on my drive to my graduate English class, I resolved to focus on Díaz's work and to seek out Latinos in genres, stories, and media where they had not been traditionally expected. This book is a part of that larger endeavor.

Many mentors, colleagues, and friends have helped shape my thinking on literature, and consequently, this book: Frederick Luis Aldama,

M. Hunter Hayes, David Herman, Brian McHale, Samuel Saldivar III, Theresa Rojas, Mary Couzelis, Andrew Spencer, J. D. Isip, Vince Liberato, Patrick Hamilton, Jesse T. Potts, Adélékè Adéèkó, Robyn Warhol, and Elizabeth Renker. Their observations and opinions have worked collectively as an intellectual grindstone that has helped sharpen my own critical instruments. My gratitude to them is beyond measure.

At Texas A&M University–Commerce, I would like to thank M. Hunter Hayes (again!) and Karen Roggenkamp for their valuable and appreciated mentorship. I am so appreciative of Donna Dunbar-Odom, Tabetha Adkins, and Christian Hemplemann, my office neighbors who are always available for much-needed perspective and assistance when I require it. And my students deserve tremendous thanks for their vigorous discussions during our explorations of Díaz's writings. I also wish to thank the helpful librarians of the James G. Gee Library for the help they provided when I needed it along the way.

At one point in the project, the kind folks at the Aragi Agency helped me locate an essay that was particularly difficult to find. They have my heartfelt appreciation.

I must thank Josh Shanholtzer and everyone involved with this project at the University of Pittsburgh Press for their hard work in shepherding this book through the publication process.

I thank my family for a lifetime of influence and motivation. Especially, I thank my brother, Robert González, who has always encouraged my academic pursuits. Because my brother attributes my passion for reading to the early intervention of Reading Is Fundamental books when I was in elementary school, I must thank this noble and worthy organization as well.

My wife, Ginger, gets the greatest share of thanks for reasons that are obvious to anyone who has been happily married for nearly two decades. My kids, Olivia and Emilia, remind me every day just how lucky I am. It is a blessing to be able to learn from them.

Finally, I thank Junot Díaz, who was so kind and encouraging when I met him in my first year of graduate school.

READING JUNOT DÍAZ

Junot Díaz has become representative of a younger generation of authors that has produced significant literary fiction in the United States in the late-twentieth and early twenty-first centuries. It is a group whose writings, for Ramón Saldívar, marks "the inauguration of a new stage in the history of the novel by twenty-first-century US ethnic writers."¹ Díaz has become an influential voice even among other notable writers such as Jonathan Lethem, Colson Whitehead, Karen Tei Yamashita, Shesshu Foster, Charles Yu, Marlon James, Edwidge Danticat, Jhumpa Lahiri, and Gary Shteyngart, to name but a few. He is the first Dominican American and only the second Latino ever to win the Pulitzer Prize for Fiction: Oscar Hijuelos (Cuban American) won in 1992 for *The Mambo Kings Play Songs of Love*. In short, Junot Díaz is currently recognized as one of the most prominent living Latino/a authors in the United States. With two story collections, a Pulitzer Prize–winning novel, and a couple of uncollected short stories to his credit, Díaz's fiction has proven to be a pivotal development not only for Latino/a writings but, perhaps more importantly, for American fiction in general.

Born on December 31, 1968, in Santo Domingo, Dominican Republic, Díaz immigrated to the United States in 1975, when he was six years old. He grew up in Perth Amboy, New Jersey, and would receive his BA from Rutgers University in New Brunswick in 1992 and his MFA from Cornell University in 1995. His first book of stories, *Drown* (1996), would effectively herald him as a new talent in American literature. A decade later his follow-up, *The Brief Wondrous Life of Oscar Wao* (2007), would earn him career-changing awards and launch Díaz as a major figure in American literature and culture. His second short story collection, *This Is How You Lose Her*, published in 2012, was a finalist for the National Book Award. Díaz would also become a creative writing professor, first at Syracuse University and then at the Massachusetts Institute of Technology. His fiction has won him numerous prestigious awards, including a Guggenheim Fellowship; the Eugene McDermott Award; the Lila Wallace–Reader's Digest Writers' Award; the PEN/Malamud Award (2002); a National Endowment for the Arts grant (2003); the John Sargent, Sr. First Novel Prize; the National Book Critics Circle Award (2007); a MacArthur Foundation "genius grant" (2012); and the *Sunday Times* EFG Private Bank Short Story Award (2013).

Díaz's turn to writing evolved over several years: "I had plans to be a teacher when I was in college, but my most secret desire . . . was really to be a writer. But I was so afraid to admit it because I thought the dreams would be smashed or I would be cheated yet again of another thing that I cared about. I think it grew so secretively."[2] Upon nearing the completion of his MFA, the publication of his first story, "Ysrael," in *Story* came at a time when he began to doubt his future as a writer: "I felt I was leaving graduate school with nothing: no stories, no agents, no interest, no confidence. . . . It was like in a movie when the hero is falling down to a certain death and suddenly reaches out and holds a branch that saves his life. That's how I felt [publishing "Ysrael"], like I grabbed a branch."[3]

In *The Norton Anthology of American Literature*, shorter eighth edition, volume two, published in 2013, the editors include for the first time a story by Díaz, "Drown." As professors view the publisher

W. W. Norton as one of the arbiters of the literature that appears in their university classrooms, Díaz's inclusion is an important and notable decision. Perhaps less a surprise is Díaz's presence in *The Norton Anthology of Latino Literature* (2011), edited by Ilan Stavans. As this essential anthology notes, "Junot Díaz was the first Dominican American man to write and publish a book-length work of fiction in English."[4] Many of Díaz's stories continue to appear in anthologies —for example, *The Scribner Anthology of Contemporary Short Fiction*, second edition; *The Art of the Story: An International Anthology of Contemporary Short Stories*; and several editions of *The Best American Short Stories*, most recently in the 2013 edition, edited by Elizabeth Strout. As editors select his stories for inclusion in more and more anthologies, his importance in considering and reevaluating conceptions of American fiction increases all the more.

Díaz's fiction has helped reset how audiences think of fiction by and about Latinos. The literary and scholarly communities have been quick to recognize Díaz's artistry. With every Díaz publication that is shortlisted and with every prize committee on which Díaz is asked to sit (such as being one of the twenty jurors for the Pulitzer Prize in 2008, the first Latino juror in the Pulitzer Prize's history), Díaz's sway in American literature grows.

This volume in the Latino and Latin American Profiles series is an opening effort to change the lack of sustained critical engagement with the entirety of Díaz's fiction. My orienting compass originates from the question of why Díaz's fiction has managed to attain such notoriety despite his use of relatively quotidian content. The substance of Díaz's stories appears unremarkable in Latino/a fiction: cheating lovers, immigration to what is believed to be a land of opportunity, escape from oppressive dictators, assimilation into white America, the clash of languages, and more. And yet Díaz can use the elements of a Latino/a narrative, say, and, through creative artistry and technique, render stories about and by Latinos in new, unexpected ways.

Indeed, it is the artful *mezcla*, or mix, of narrative design and Latino culture that makes Díaz's fiction so potent, as well as his ability to "change our perspective on the Americas by offering a narrative from a 'periphery' which becomes the center."[5] At the level of storytelling convention, Díaz's is often guided by the principle of rule breaking in creating his fiction.

This is not to say that his stories are amorphous or somehow lack a purposeful storyworld design. On the contrary, Díaz has stated that his ability to publish quickly is blunted by his careful and deliberate approach to writing:

> I'm a slow writer. Which is bad enough but given that I'm in a world where it's considered abnormal if a writer *doesn't* produce a book every year or two—it makes me look even worse. Ultimately [*The Brief Wondrous Life of Oscar Wao*] wouldn't have it any other way. This book wanted x number of years out of my life. Perhaps I could have written a book in a shorter time but it wouldn't have been this book and this was the book I wanted to write. Other reasons? I'm a crazy perfectionist. I suffer from crippling bouts of depression. I write two score pages for every one I keep.[6]

When Díaz deploys his narrator of choice, Yunior de Las Casas, there is an apparent free-flowing nature to his fiction that seems like someone speaking to an interlocutor. But there is also precision in Díaz's creation of story as well. His stories often rely on the sort of precise timing one finds in a stand-up comedy routine, a skill evinced by many authors writing in the early twenty-first century such as Gary Shteyngart and Colson Whitehead, whose works of fiction are also examples of the resplendent and exquisite timing of humor in recent ethnic American fiction. In short, this book pays critical attention to Díaz's fiction with the aim of illuminating its purposeful storyworld designs (formal features), its engagement with audiences (on emotional and cognitive levels), and contexts within American culture (broadly defined).

One final caveat before delving into Díaz's carefully crafted story-worlds. Scholars of Latino/a literature often approach their subject by concentrating on the ideopolitical valences that bear out in such writings. Indeed, this critical stance is a valuable contribution to our understanding of what we call Latino/a literature and the authors who belong to that highly diverse group identified as Latinos. Latino/a literature often apprises readers regarding matters of Latino/a culture —from family dynamics, to religious practices, to the significance of particular foods, to political issues of immigration, to the "whitening" of Latinos in the United States—even if that is not its overt agenda. However, the narrative design of Latino/a fiction works as a delivery system for these important ideopolitical matters. Thus, this book seeks to give equal consideration to form and design as a means of better understanding the cultural and thematic concerns that resonate within Díaz's fiction. The thematics of his fiction are not novel; rather, it is the way in which he structures his storyworlds that elevates Díaz's fiction. It seems that what makes Junot Díaz "Junot Díaz" is less a matter of what issues he deals with and more a matter of how he articulates the design of his respective storyworlds. Indeed, readers are challenged, and at times are confronted, by narrative issues that arise precisely as a result of creative decisions Díaz makes. Rather than consider the elements of narrative in his fiction as secondary to Díaz's artistry, this book adopts the position that, in the case of Díaz's fiction in particular, it is valuable to give equitable consideration to formal matters of design in a scholarly examination of his work as a means of elucidating the thematic content.

THE CHANGING LATINO DEMOGRAPHIC

Junot Díaz belongs to a group of Latino/a writers whose dates and places of birth distinguish them from earlier groundbreaking authors in the field. This younger group of writers includes Daniel Alarcón, Salvador Plascencia, Reyna Grande, Loida Maritza Pérez, and others who were both born around or after the US Civil Rights Movement and outside of the United States. Unlike Latinos who were writing of the experience of a second- or third-generation Latino or Latina during a national push for civil rights—writers such as Rudolfo Anaya and Oscar "Zeta" Acosta in the early 1970s and Chicana feminists Gloria Anzaldúa and Sandra Cisneros in the 1980s—Díaz is an immigrant from the Dominican Republic who brings with him a global, geopolitical sensibility to his craft. His transnational worldview is a critical detail to understanding his fiction, one that I will explore in depth below but will preview briefly here. Works of the so-called Chicano Renaissance often showcase a storyworld that unfolds in a precise geographic location and concentrates on issues of cultural tradition, language, and social hegemony. Even authors such as Julia Alvarez, Achy Obejas, and Cristina García—authors who, like Díaz, were born outside of the United States and emigrated as young children—craft narratives that penetrate matters of history and cultural identity by unifying the American experience with the Latin American experience. They reveal a Latino/a sensibility intimately connected with the fatherlands and motherlands of their past, what José David Saldívar identifies as "trans-Americanity."[7]

In short, the Latino/a community of today is not the homogenized group of brown people envisioned by the Eisenhower-era "Operation Wetback." The rapid expansion of the Latino population in border states such as Texas, California, and Arizona as well as in the midwestern states of Michigan, Nebraska, and Ohio and the southern states of Alabama and North Carolina suggests a community that is growing not simply in number but in diversity as well. The *guatemaltecos* of LA are meeting the Cuban Americans of Miami and the Dominicans of Paterson, New Jersey, in the heartland of America. Just as the Latino/a demographic demonstrates the varied nature of this expansion of people and culture, the literature now being produced by this younger generation of Latinos further underscores the plurality of Latino/a experience. What is more, Latino/a authors themselves are pushing against simple categorizations of their work by diversifying the kinds of narratives they write and the structures their stories take. Coupled with a readership that is receptive to these recent Latino/a stories as never before, the expansion of Latino/a literature is poised to mirror the increase of Latinos themselves.

Unlike the majority of Latino/a writers who were either self-taught or learned to write in other disciplines such as law (Oscar "Zeta" Acosta), education (Tomás Rivera), or folkloric studies (Américo Paredes), Díaz is the product of the MFA system of writing in the United States. His culminating project in the MFA program at Cornell University would ultimately become his pathbreaking collection of stories, *Drown*. Although this is now a conventional route writers take to becoming published authors, such a path to publication is relatively recent among Latino/a writers. One early notable Latino/a writer to rise through the MFA system is Sandra Cisneros, who received her MFA from the University of Iowa in 1978. But take stock of Latino/a authors since 1978 and you will find relatively few Latinos that have gone the route of the MFA. I take particular note of this issue because, for many American writers who end up as career authors, the MFA is the de facto path for becoming this sort of writer. For Latinos, the MFA has only recently become such a viable option. Díaz himself has noted the nearly accidental manner in which he entered the MFA program at Cornell, how he applied "blindly and not very widely" to "six programs, and out of some blind pocket of luck that the Universe reserves for total fools I got into one: Cornell."[8] Though his talent is not accidental, his taking the writing path via an MFA is an outlier in more ways than one.

Despite what such an opportunity might indicate to the layperson, Díaz's time in the MFA program at Cornell was not the sort of creative flowering writing workshops are often imagined to be. Díaz is highly, severely critical of his experience at Cornell, which he now recounts as exalting white male experience as a default narrative setting, where it was unproblematic for a white writer to write of diverse characters. Meanwhile, writers of color were discouraged from creating distinct worlds in their writing. Díaz recalls with a tone of regret how several excellent writers of color ultimately left the program because of the hostility they faced. He laments one particular writer whom he identifies as "Athena" who had had enough and left the program.[9] Her writing has left an indelible mark on his memory.

Such criticisms of MFA programs by writers of color—and Latino/a writers especially, is not new. For years Sandra Cisneros, the prizewinning author of *The House on Mango Street*, *Woman Hollering Creek*, and *Caramelo* has lambasted the Iowa Writers' Workshop for many of the same reasons Díaz excoriates his experience at Cornell. For Cisneros, not only were the students pressured to consider the white American experience as the default, normal position, her identity status as a Chicana with empowered notions of feminism were unwelcome in her program. Regarding the prestigious Iowa Writers' Workshop, she states, "It wasn't so prestigious to me. It was rather horrible. I like to tell people that I'm a writer despite the University of Iowa Writers' Workshop. It taught me what I didn't want to be as a writer and how I didn't want to teach." When the interviewer says, "It sounds like you absolutely hated it," Cisneros responds, "Well, that's putting it mildly, yes."[10] Díaz has expressed a similar view regarding his MFA experience.

Indeed, one criticism of the MFA system of writing is that it homogenizes writers too stringently, that it doesn't leave enough room for conceiving of and nurturing a type of writing that lies outside of that *New Yorker* style of narrative. In Díaz's case, he blends the highbrow aspirations of "literature" with so-called lowbrow forms of popular culture such as comic books and the rhythmic yet gritty vernacular of the inner city. Unlike those Chicano/a writers who have danced with folklore, mysticism, and magical realism for decades, Díaz arises nearly *ex nihilo* as a Latino/a writer. That is to say, one is more apt to find antecedents for his style of fiction in the works of David Foster Wallace or Michael Chabon than of Rudolfo Anaya or even fellow Pulitzer Prize–winner Oscar Hijuelos. This point is most easily grasped when considering Díaz's ideal audience—an audience that understands the dynamics of a Dominican family as quickly as it understands the science fictions of Samuel R. Delany, Octavia Butler, and Gene Wolfe.

That is not to say that Díaz does not owe a literary debt of gratitude to Latino/a writers who have come before him. For example, he has on several occasions praised Cisneros, whose works he came to know during his college years.[11] But in addition to Cisneros, Díaz also acknowledges how the works of Leslie Marmon Silko, and especially those of Toni Morrison and Octavia Butler, proved to be a monumental influence on him and his work. These profound works not only were evidence of the technical craft of literature but were also, for Díaz, proof positive that writers of color could create influential works, and that those works could hold sway over a younger generation of writers. Call it the literary version of paying it forward. His stories have already made a lasting impact on Latino/a literature as well as American literature. Perhaps most importantly, however, his works have managed to bridge the chasm between Latino/a culture and the American pop cultural imagination.

At least two defining traits in Díaz's fiction distinguish it from other exemplars of Latino/a literature. The first is his use of language. Code-switching and the problems inherent in its use in fiction have long been a part of world literature, and, in this case, Latino/a literature. For many early writers of Latino/a heritage, Spanish was often the language of the home, of familial interaction. Spanish, as spoken in the homes of Hispanic American families, was and continues to be a living thing. It is quite often slangy and colloquial—including certain words not to be found in Spanish dictionaries overseen by the Real Academia Español, the organization that declares official Spanish words. On the contrary, Spanish in the United States has taken on a life of its own, as one would expect from living languages. And with Spanish speakers working and living in a predominantly English-speaking culture in America, we also see "Spanglish," which

Ilan Stavans has written about extensively. He provides a pithy but fruitful definition for this blending of the two languages that indicates a fusion of culture: "*Spanglish*, n. The verbal encounter between Anglo and Hispano civilizations."[12] For Díaz, his refusal to designate the Spanish words in his fiction as somehow different via italics or quotation marks is a political decision: "Spanish is not a minority language. Not in this hemisphere, not in the United States, not in the world inside my head. So why treat it like one? Why 'other' it? Why denormalize it? . . . I want to remind readers of the fluidity of languages, the mutability of languages. And to mark how steadily English is transforming Spanish and Spanish is transforming English."[13]

Díaz is certainly not the first to code-switch or use many linguistic codes alternately in his fiction. Even in what is often called the first Latino/a novel, *Pocho*, by José Antonio Villarreal, published in 1959, there is a great deal of code-switching and alternating use of the English and Spanish languages. However, *Pocho* and many other code-switching narratives like it almost always use Spanish with an English-only reader in mind. That is to say, whenever an author uses Spanish, there follows an immediate translation into English. In the case of *Pocho*, Villarreal translates Spanish spoken by the characters in an English that, in its attempts to be faithful to the source, comes across as stilted and awkward to an English-language reader. Or, as in Piri Thomas's *Down These Mean Streets*, sometimes a glossary is appended to the narrative proper. In short, Díaz's use of Spanish is not in and of itself a novel innovation. Rather, his decision to use Spanish without much consideration for a reader that does not understand Spanish is key. Instead of providing a glossary or translating the Spanish he uses, Díaz allows the Spanish to stand for itself. As Rune Graulund asserts, "Díaz implements a politics of exclusion [in *Oscar Wao*], actively forcing his readers to accept that parts of his text will likely remain indecipherable to them."[14] To be sure, a reader can correctly deduce a lot of the Spanish by using contextual clues, but not all of it, creating a potentially volatile relationship between reader and text.

The second defining trait is related to the first. Díaz brings together Latino/a culture, and specifically Dominican American culture, with many aspects of popular culture. Because speculative fiction, film, and television—science fiction, fantasy, and superhero comics—so profoundly influenced him as they have many other American authors such as Michael Chabon and Jonathan Lethem, it is hardly a wonder that such references and allusions appear within Díaz's fiction. But these allusions, often dropped in without citation or explanation, can create a distancing effect for the reader similar to that which is caused by Spanish that may not be understood.

Taken together, these defining traits, as I have called them, have several important implications for Latino/a literature. To begin with, it shows what many Latino/a authors have argued all along; that is, that readers, and, in this case, *willing* readers, will find that a sprinkling of untranslated Spanish will not hinder them. Historically, authors make concessions to publishers no matter their heritage or identity. But Latino/a writers have often been forced to make many more concessions in their writings, and those concessions often have to do with language and how writers use it. The success of Díaz's writings is proof that readers are far more capable than many publishers give them credit for. It is also evidence of a burgeoning audience that is hungry for sophisticated fiction by and about Latinos.

In addition, because Díaz's fiction weaves the gritty realism of urban Latinidad together with the fantastical worldviews of speculative fiction, it has the effect of uncoupling Latino/a culture from the powerful influence of the stereotype. As William Anthony Nericcio has shown, the appropriation of the Mexican stereotype in America —to sell tacos (Taco Bell), to entertain children (*Looney Tunes*'s Speedy Gonzales), to entice and enthrall audiences (e.g., Rita Hayworth, Mexican *bandidos*, etc.)—continues with little abatement.

Such stereotypes are so powerful and damaging because they become entrenched in the psyche of mainstream America.[15] So, when Díaz opens his novel *The Brief Wondrous Life of Oscar Wao* with an epigraph quoting Stan Lee and Jack Kirby's *The Fantastic Four* comic book, it breaks new ground for where Latino/a literature can go. It also fights the simplistic conceptions that pervade discussions of Latinos in the United States as well. As Stavans states in *The Norton Anthology of Latino Literature* regarding *Oscar Wao*, "Díaz's vision represents a break not only from the traditional acculturation story, but also from the ethnic novel. . . . Díaz reflects on the way popular culture defines youth in the United States."[16] In short, Díaz's rise as a prominent literary figure in America is indicative of and coincides with the changing Latino/a demographic in the United States. In what follows, I examine Díaz's fiction within the three books he has published to date, in the order of their publication, as well as some of his selected uncollected fiction and nonfiction.

CHAPTER I

Drown
(1996)

For analytical purposes, I have organized the stories in *Drown* into groups that share certain characteristics, such as a dominant theme or character. I have done this rather than take the stories in the order that they appear for several reasons. First, despite the fact that many of the stories orbit Yunior's sphere of experience, much of the underlying detail comes to the surface only when juxtaposing particular stories. Take, for example, the two stories that prominently feature the character known as Ysrael, the Dominican boy whose face was mauled and disfigured by a pig when he was an infant. In "Ysrael" he is the object of Yunior's fascination and Rafa's torment while in "No Face" Ysrael is the protagonist of the story. These are the first and penultimate stories as they appear in the book, respectively. I have brought the stories together in my analysis and have treated them as something of a unit.[1]

"YSRAEL" AND "NO FACE"

Though these two stories are not explicitly about Yunior's father, there appear what I call "shadow fathers" who work as stand-in father figures, such as Yunior's older brother Rafa. Or there is the mention of fathers who are supposedly toiling away in a distant America in order to bring the rest of their families to join them once they have earned

enough money. "Ysrael" and "No Face" are as much about Yunior's
development vis-à-vis his father's absence as they are about the disfigured Ysrael. Yunior's curiosity for Ysrael begins as typical childish
naïveté but quickly becomes something approaching monstrous in
"Ysrael," thanks in large measure to Rafa's cruelty. In "No Face," the
disfigured boy, a superhero in his own mind, reveals the bravery of a
boy with an identity crisis.

The opening story, "Ysrael," establishes many of the themes
teased out and illuminated in Díaz's later writings. The troubled
relationship between brothers, the compulsion and consequences
of adhering to machismo scripts, the poignancy of being an outcast
in your own community, the lack of an engaging father in a boy's
life, and the harsh realities faced by so many children all resonate in
Díaz's later fiction. "Children are not treated like the future," Díaz
laments; "They're exploited, they're abused, they're raped, they're
killed."[2] *Drown* destroys the notion of idyllic spaces where children
live trauma-free. Yunior is the narrator of "Ysrael," so the story is also
a reader's introduction to the dominant narrative voice throughout
Díaz's fiction. John Riofrio notes that the story also "sets the stage
for the picture of masculinity which will reveal itself throughout all
ten of the stories."[3] Here, Yunior is a nine-year-old boy, still in the
Dominican Republic, at a point in his life where he is already on
the verge of adulthood. Yunior has had to grow up fast, just as his
brother Rafa has had to do. As we find out in later stories such as
"Aguantando," Yunior has had to do without his father for most of
his first nine years. Though Rafa is only three years older than Yunior
and just on the cusp of pubescence himself, he looms over Yunior as
a much wiser, less patient mentor. Though the dynamic between the
two brothers will wax and wane in subsequent stories, there is already
a seemingly insuperable gulf between them in this initial story. It is
a distance between the brothers that will persist until Rafa dies, and
arguably even after his death.

At its core the story is about discovery and violation, and how the two are often part and parcel of one another. The two brothers are bored because their mother has sent them to the campo to stay with their uncles while she works long hours in the chocolate factory. Without the daily distractions they would typically find in their barrio in Santo Domingo, Yunior and Rafa are forced to find other ways to alleviate the boredom. Rafa often tells Yunior about the girls he has been with, but he never lets his younger brother come with him on his excursions of sexual conquest. In fact, Rafa teases Yunior when they are together in public spaces, calling him "Señor Haitian" in front of their friends back in Santo Domingo. "In the Capital Rafa and I fought so much that our neighbors took to smashing broomsticks over us to break it up, but in the campo it wasn't like that. In the campo we were friends," Yunior notes.[4] "Ysrael was a different story," because Rafa allows Yunior to go with him to see Ysrael's misshapen face. But in order to discover what Ysrael looks like under his homespun blue mask, the brothers must violate Ysrael's personal space and dignity. Yunior does not yet grasp this, but Rafa does. This bit of knowledge evinces the difference between the two brothers.

As a narrator, one of Yunior's personal quirks is that the subjects of his stories tend to be either himself or an outcast figure that he knows or has known personally. When he's not talking about his experiences, he's recounting events concerning persons marginalized within their community. In this story, for instance, the title character has become an object of mystification and ridicule through no fault of his own. A pig entered Ysrael's house when he was a baby and managed to chew off parts of his face before anyone noticed. Later, Oscar de León, another outcast figure, will become the subject of the novel *The Brief Wondrous Life of Oscar Wao*.

Most of the events that make up "Ysrael" take place over the course of one day, with occasional flashbacks to Yunior's previous interactions with Ysrael. There is a series of obstacles the brothers must overcome to see what lies hidden beneath Ysrael's mask. In this respect the story is reminiscent of the challenge presented to the heroes of classical Greek myth—Jason's taking of the golden fleece, Heracles's taking of the golden apples, and so on. The quest to see Ysrael's face is a challenge to Yunior's development from a naïve boy to a streetwise player like Rafa. Robbing Ysrael of his privacy and dignity may not make a man of Yunior, but it goes a long way toward establishing his machismo bona fides, particularly in the eyes of his older brother. Rafa figuratively takes Yunior to school. He shows him how to get money by exchanging Coca-Cola bottles that belong to their tío, how to scam the cobrador on the bus, and how to sneak up on someone as formidable as the Minotaur-like Ysrael in order to remove his mask. The disparity between Yunior's naïveté and Rafa's experience appears to be much more than three years would suggest.

A masculine script motivates Yunior's world, and he must come to terms with it. It is a world where one is either the violator or the violated. He learns this lesson twofold on the day they go to see Ysrael. The first lesson occurs while he and Rafa are on the bus. While Rafa is hustling the cobrador by confusing him, a pedophile touches Yunior's private area in the public space of the bus. A grease stain has formed on the outside of Yunior's pants, the result of stashing a pastelito in his pocket. As he begins to wipe it, an old man begins to help him wipe the stain, only to begin touching Yunior's penis. Though Yunior berates the man, calling him a "pato," he is clearly traumatized by the experience. When the brothers bolt without paying their fare and are safe in a field, Yunior begins to cry. The encounter leaves Yunior shaken, but Rafa thinks it is because they didn't pay the bus fare. "You," Rafa says, "are a pussy" (13). And later, "Are you always going to be a pussy?" (14). Yunior cannot answer, and he cannot tell Rafa what happened back on the bus. According to Rafa, the appropriate response to trauma is to "get tougher" (14).

The second lesson Yunior learns occurs with the removal of Ysrael's mask. While Rafa knows exactly the scheme he is pulling on Ysrael, Yunior begins to form what might be an actual friendship with Ysrael. They both have an interest in wrestling, and they both have absent fathers currently in the United States. Just as Yunior notices that Ysrael is smiling beneath his mask, Rafa smashes a Coke bottle on Ysrael's head. The sight of Ysrael's face frightens Yunior when he and Rafa remove the mask, and the story closes with Yunior's concern for the violated boy, a boy not unlike himself, a boy that very easily might have been Yunior.

Rafa destroys any illusions that somehow Ysrael "will be OK" when Yunior suggests it at the end of the story (19). Nearly all of Díaz's fiction concerns Yunior to some degree, even when the story is not overtly about him. That is to say, even stories about other characters that are narrated by Yunior are in many ways about his development and maturation. The Coke bottle smashed over Ysrael's head operates like some terrible enlightenment for Yunior and the other male characters in *Drown*, where "empathy is a dangerous and problematic sentiment."[5] The world is not a place where the deserving always triumph. It is a world that is ever poised to blindside you. This stunning revelation announces Yunior's entrance into manhood.

While "Ysrael" is Yunior's initiation into a world of cruelty, misfortune, and loss, "No Face" is narrated in third person with Ysrael as the protagonist. Though the story never identifies Ysrael as the character known as No Face, certain personality traits readily identify him as the same disfigured boy. Yunior is nowhere to be found within the story. And yet, because "No Face" appears as the penultimate story in *Drown*, we feel Yunior's presence just beyond the margins of the page. His first experience with Ysrael (we never find out if there are other moments where the two interact) is merely an introduction. Indeed, much of Ysrael remains unknown both to readers and to Yunior.

It is important to note that in "No Face" Ysrael is the focalizer, and the story is all about him. In "Ysrael" Yunior and Rafa objectify Ysrael. Specifically, Rafa smashes any possibility that Ysrael and Yunior might develop a friendship. The masked boy who flew kites and loved to wrestle remained little more than an opportunity for Yunior, as a writer, to learn something of himself. "No Face," however, shows us Ysrael less as an object and more as a fully realized person with the hopes, aspirations, and dreams of his youth still vibrant and tantalizingly within reach. Ironically, Ysrael still can claim an innocent, less jaded view of the world when compared to Yunior. In "Ysrael," Rafa is confident in the knowledge that Ysrael will remain disfigured for the rest of his days. In "No Face," Ysrael has no reason to doubt that doctors might surgically repair his face one day. At least not yet.

"No Face" also marks Díaz's first foray into the realm of superheroic comic book figures in his fiction—something that comes to the fore in *The Brief Wondrous Life of Oscar Wao*. Ysrael uses his disfigurement, and especially his homemade mask, to create a superhero persona for himself called No Face. His daily routine and interactions with his community are all filtered through the persona people call No Face. He "grinds his fist into his palm" when he puts on the mask each morning and runs in dynamic fashion past "drunks" and "pissholes" as a matter of daily business (153–54). He grunts in dissatisfaction at the cleaning woman who tells him to go away. When she asks if he has any shame, he "grip[s] the bars of the gate and pull[s] them a bit apart, grunting, to show her who she was messing with" (155). Significantly, every week Padre Lou allows him to purchase a comic book. In the story, he buys the comic of the turban-wearing Kaliman.

Indeed, Díaz engages several tropes of popular culture in "No Face." The protagonist wears a mask and is a fierce fan of wrestling, a nod to the Latin American style of wrestling known as lucha libre and one of its most notable figures, El Santo. Lucha libre is different from the American brand of "wrestling entertainment"; El Santo, for example, carried his masked persona into films where he was a crime fighter. No Face patterns himself after El Santo and superheroes like Kaliman, and the desire to fight evil shapes his identity. He invokes the words "FLIGHT" and "STRENGTH" at critical moments, and Díaz stylizes these words in all caps as an indication of their incantatory power. No Face completes certain daily routines that contribute to his superhero persona, and the fact that people in town identify him as No Face and not his actual name underscores his superheroic sensibilities.

In reality, however, No Face is a pariah and a constant target for bullies, continuing the sort of abuses he endures in "Ysrael." In that story Yunior himself admits that the previous summer he had "pegged Ysrael with a rock" and "clocked his shoulder blade" (14). In "No Face," four boys ambush Ysrael and taunt him mercilessly. When one of the boys pins No Face to the ground, it is reminiscent of the helplessness Ysrael experienced during the life-defining moment when the pig mauled parts of his face. He often has nightmares where he must relive the mauling again and again.

Though his disfigurement is not congenital, there are several interesting parallels to another famous deformed pariah in literature: Victor Hugo's infamous bell ringer, Quasimodo. No Face and Quasimodo both find sanctuary in a house of worship and are of uncommon strength. No Face has a kind father figure named Padre Lou, a local priest who cares for him and teaches him bits of English. Padre Lou is the only character in either story who seems to care altruistically for Ysrael, even more than his family.

But it will take a great deal of money to repair the damage done to Ysrael's face. In each story, there is the indication that two "fathers" are working to make the surgery a reality. In "Ysrael," we discover that Ysrael's father is in New York, but in "No Face" his father is at home. It is not easy to discern which story occurs first, though there is something ominous about his father's presence at home. That Padre Lou has taken it upon himself to help Ysrael is notable. It may be an indication that Ysrael's father is no longer in a position to live up to his son's hopes for the surgical repair of his face. Near the end of "No Face," his mother sees him outside early one morning and tells him to leave before his father sees him. No Face "knows what happens when his father comes out" (160). In "Ysrael" there is a sense of pride in father and son—his father supposedly purchased in New York the very kite Ysrael flies. However, in "No Face" Ysrael has left his literal father for his spiritual one. After the ostensible financial failures of his biological father, Ysrael delights in his imaginary No Face persona as he turns to superhero narratives and religious hope to get him through the morass of daily life. He is a local boy whose only chance at being restored is to make it to Canada or the United States.

In these two stories, Díaz explores the consequences of absent fathers and the well-meaning surrogates who take their places in the lives of young, hopeful, yet impressionable boys. In the many stories that follow, Yunior will prove to be shaped by Rafa's influence as much as by their father's absence. Young Dominican boys confront significant challenges early in life, and Ysrael's disfigurement as an infant works as a potent metaphor in this regard. Admirably, Ysrael works hard at fortifying his self-confidence and identity around that which makes him the object of ridicule and mystery—his disfigurement and his mask, respectively. Yunior proves to be heavily influenced by his older brother, and Rafa's tutelage arguably results in many emotionally painful events in Yunior's life. Both boys will ultimately work to improve their physical abilities. Ysrael is a devotee of wrestling and does various crude exercises to increase his strength and speed, while Yunior reveals in *The Brief Wondrous Life of Oscar Wao* that he lifts weights. Deficiencies in their emotional well-being motivate their turn to physical improvement. The two will also turn out to be shaped by storytelling. No matter how fast he is—and in "No Face" we're told "nobody's faster" (160)—Ysrael can never outrun the telling and retelling of how the pig walked right into the house and chewed off half of his face, nor can he forget the memory of it. Yunior becomes a writer whose entire corpus appears to be about himself and pariah figures, such as Oscar de León and Belicia Cabral, and Ysrael in *Drown*'s opening story.

Yunior leaves the carefree world of his childhood for good the instant Rafa wrests Ysrael's flea-ridden mask from his face and Yunior gazes at the lasting injuries. When he surveys Ysrael's face, he observes, "His left ear was a nub and you could see the thick veined slab of his tongue through a hole in his cheek. He had no lips. His head was tipped back and his eyes had gone white and the cords were out on his neck. He'd been an infant when the pig had come into the house. The damage looked old but I still jumped back and said, Please Rafa, let's go!" (19). The revelation of Ysrael's destroyed face scars Yunior emotionally. As he grows into adulthood, this signature moment shapes what Yunior finds worthy of a story. It's not a difficult leap to believe that "No Face" is a story written by Yunior much later in life. Just as he is compelled to write Oscar's story as *The Brief Wondrous Life of Oscar Wao*, he is moved to preserve the idea of Ysrael as a superhero. Far from being disfigured by reeling from the cruelties of bullies, No Face forever outruns his foes and continually fights the evil he encounters in life. Yunior's writing has the power to give his subjects that which they lacked in life, allowing them to face life in a way they never could have done in reality.

"FIESTA, 1980," "AGUANTANDO," AND "NEGOCIOS"

A notable aspect of *Drown* is the number of stories that trace the absence of Yunior's father, Ramón de Las Casas, in Yunior's life. "Fiesta, 1980," "Aguantando," and "Negocios" are a trio of stories that relate the pain and hurt of a young boy who does not have his father at home during the formative years of his life. If the three stories are read in the order in which they appear, they are out of chronological order. Later I will provide my rationale as to why the stories appear so in the volume. Here I will concentrate on that which unites the three stories as a unit—that is, besides Yunior—Yunior's father, Ramón.

Yunior's relationship with his father is, at best, estranged throughout much of their lives. These three stories show the uncertainty and self-imposed guilt children often feel when they have absentee parents. In "Aguantando" Yunior struggles with his father's absence, and in "Fiesta, 1980" one clearly sees the tension between the two of them after their reunion in the United States. Upon reaching adulthood,

Yunior can ask the sort of questions he couldn't when he was a boy.
Yunior narrates those painful years when he was in the Dominican
Republic wondering why Ramón had forgotten him and his family. In "Negocios," incidentally one of the longest in either *Drown*
or *This Is How You Lose Her*, Yunior employs his skill as a storyteller.
He entices his readers to view his story as a redemptive (or at least
somewhat recuperative) act on behalf of his father, with whom he
struggled to get along for so long. I begin my discussion of these three
stories with "Negocios" because it will help address certain unknowns
in the other two stories.

As with many translated words, *negocios* can have several meanings. It can mean "business," as in "taking care of one's business." It
can also refer to a business that can be managed and owned. A third
connotation for *negocios* is "affairs"—a word that alludes to Ramón's
extramarital behavior, and later, the behavior of his sons Rafa and
Yunior. In many ways "Negocios" helps provide a context for, or at the
least a rationale of, Yunior's proclivities when it comes to his relationships with women.

The first striking aspect of this story is that Yunior narrates it but
often seems to know the thoughts and feelings of other characters
that only they could know. This situation begs the question of how
Yunior could know all of this regarding his father, when he was in a
different country and when Yunior was just a child. In one revealing
moment in the story, Yunior notes that Papi (his father) is the source
of his information:

> Nobody bought coats then, Papi told me, because nobody was expect-
> ing to stay that long. So I kept going back and any chance I got I
> kissed her. She would tense up and tell me to leave, like I'd hit her.
> So I would kiss her again and she'd say, Oh, I really think you better
> leave now. She was a crazy lady. I kept it up and one day she kissed
> me back. Finally. By then I knew every maldito train in the city and
> I had this big wool coat and two pairs of gloves. I looked like an
> Eskimo. Like an American. (186)

At some point, it seems, Ramón related many of his experiences to Yunior, and Yunior took the information and created a story. As a narrator, Yunior allows his father's words to come through unmediated and unfiltered. Yunior narrates as if he is a third-person narrator with Ramón as focalizer until the last section, where Yunior takes the prominent position of the first-person narrator.

"Negocios" is an example of how Díaz can amplify certain attributes of his stories through choices in narrative structure and narrator. Quite easily, he might have used a third-person narrator, as he did in "No Face," in order to tell the story of a particular character. But such a decision would nullify much of the emotional significance of these three stories. "Fiesta, 1980" and "Aguantando" portray Ramón as an authoritarian who is unfaithful to his family. To have "Negocios" narrated by anyone other than Yunior would have yielded a sappy and unconvincing corrective to the character we thought we knew and had come to dislike so well. Díaz devises a story that allows Yunior the catharsis of recuperating his father while having the added benefit of ameliorating Ramón, at least to a small degree, in the eyes of the reader.

On the other hand, Yunior doesn't tell his father's story in a way that makes Ramón a saint. Again this reveals why Yunior is an apt narrator for "Negocios." If there is anything that characterizes Yunior as a narrator, it's that he is brutally honest and has a razor-sharp wit. Thus, readers can take it that by voicing his father's side of the story, Yunior is not absolving Ramón of the mistakes he made in his life. It does help Yunior understand the many challenges his papi faced and overcame. Yunior can only come to such an understanding after he has become a man himself and has repeated many of the same sorts of mistakes.

Before Ramón left for the United States, he was already guilty of having an affair. This characteristic of being a cheater appears to be a genetic defect, for it is something Yunior—named after Ramón—will struggle with throughout many of his narratives. There remains, how-

ever, some ambiguity as to Ramón's motivations. Does he leave for the
United States in order to create a better life for his wife, Virta, and his
two sons? Or does he simply need a reason to get away from Virta?
The ability to discern Ramón's intentions remains out of Yunior's, and
subsequently the reader's, grasp.

Yunior begins "Negocios" by saying that his father "left Santo
Domingo just before my fourth birthday" (163). For five long years
Ramón remains as an ephemeral figure in Yunior's imagination; that
five-year period is the subject of "Aguantando." Once he can do so,
Yunior sets down his father's story of this missing time by highlight-
ing the hardships Ramón faced once he landed in Miami. Ramón's
determination and work ethic are manifest in his struggle to find and
keep employment as well as in his efforts to learn English. He is sub-
jected to hard times and robbery, but also some good fortune along
the way. As his sons will do later, Ramón finds himself in a relationship with a woman named Nilda, a woman who very nearly makes
Ramón forget about his family back in the Dominican Republic. In
fact, Ramón has a son with Nilda and names him Ramón, making
this baby the third Ramón (Yunior is the second). At times, Ramón
slips and calls his latest child "Yunior," which incenses Nilda, and
in effect erases the original Yunior's identity, as if he doesn't exist
or is illegitimate. When his relationship with Nilda progressively
degrades, Ramón finally returns to get his family.

After Yunior finally meets Nilda in her home one day after
Ramón "had left us for good" (206), he empathizes with her because
he knows full well what it means to be abandoned by someone you
love. During the time Ramón was struggling in the United States,
Yunior was growing up without a father in the Dominican Republic, as "Aguantando" reveals. One might translate the story's title as
"surviving," which reveals the hole in Yunior's life created by Ramón's
absence. "I lived without a father for the first nine years of my life,"
the story opens. "He was in the States, working, and the only way I
knew him was through the photographs my moms kept in a plastic

sandwich bag under her bed" (69). The story highlights the crucial period leading up to the moment Ramón returns for his family and, importantly, is from Yunior's perspective.

In "Aguantando" Yunior takes on precisely what his father's absence meant to him. For much of Yunior's life, Ramón is a washed-out figure in sepia photographs stored in a plastic bag. Because Yunior lives in such impoverished conditions while his father is in the United States, the implication is that the family's economic struggles are Ramón's fault: "We didn't eat rocks but we didn't eat meat or beans, either. . . . When me and Rafa caught our annual case of worms it was only by skimping on our dinners that Mami could afford to purchase the Verminox. I can't remember how many times I crouched over our latrine, my teeth clenched, watching long gray parasites slide out from between my legs" (71). Yunior's sufferings are ironic in light of what we learn of Ramón in "Negocios"; Ramón's very reason for leaving for the United States is so he can provide his family with a better life. He does indeed succeed in this endeavor, though it takes him no less than five years to bring his grand scheme to fruition.

The distance between Ramón and his family, particularly Yunior, results in a deep poverty that serves as a constant reminder that the head of the household is the cause of the situation. During the intervening years, Yunior notices Rafa enjoys being away from his family—already the older son is taking after his father. But Yunior takes the opposite approach: "I never wanted to be away from the family. Intuitively, I knew how easily distances could harden and become permanent" (75). Quite often in stories that feature Yunior, the de Las Casas men follow in their father's figurative footsteps—as cheaters.

Unfortunately, because of the lack of money, "when times were real flojo" (74), Yunior and Rafa were sent to live temporarily with members of their extended family. The second section of the story depicts this fear of separation when Yunior expresses his trepidation while Rafa expresses only excitement at having to leave home. Yunior cannot reveal his true feelings here, which is another characteristic of his many narratives. In "Aguantando," he must feign a blasé attitude when he finds his mother and Rafa have returned to take him home: "You're back, I'd say, trying to hide the excitement in my voice" (76). The section closes with the image of silent affection between two brothers. Yunior describes this meaningful, if incomplete, reunion: "I'd sit next to him and he'd put his arm around me and we'd listen to Tía telling Mami how well I behaved and all the different things I'd eaten" (77). The scene is a fleeting shade of a stable family structure, but it is one that will not obtain.

Upon the arrival of a letter from Ramón, the family is thrust into chaos. Unlike Rafa, Yunior cannot understand what has upset their mother. When Rafa reveals to Yunior that the letter states that Ramón will soon return, he tempers his younger brother's excitement by reminding him that their father has made this promise before many times. In a flashback, Yunior recalls those other times his father had announced his imminent return and the horrible disappointment that followed. Yunior has the luxury of not remembering his emotional longing to see his father due to his youth. His relationship with his father comes only in the form of looking at Ramón's pictures. Because Yunior cannot remember the events concerning their father, it is notable that Rafa is the bearer of this family record. In addition, Rafa can read—something Yunior is unable to do even at the age of nine. Their mother never talks about Ramón or the pain he has caused, making Rafa's recollections all the more important for Yunior. The story further reinforces the bond between the two brothers.

Interestingly, Ramón's return is never depicted in "Aguantando." The story is entirely made up of life during his absence, right up to the moment of the reunion itself. Rather than relate the actual reunion, Yunior narrates his fantasy version of how his father would return. He idealizes the moment in prose by revealing how he had always hoped and imagined his reunion with his father might be. In Yunior's imagination, Ramón would see his youngest son and say

"What's wrong with that one?" Their reunion—an introduction, as far as Yunior is concerned—is a wonderfully wrought moment of filial love: "Squatting down so that his pale yellow socks showed, he'd trace the scars on my arms and on my head. Yunior, he'd finally say, his stubbled face in front of mine, his thumb tracing a circle on my cheek" (88). There is something poignant about what Ramón does to Yunior at this moment, an indication that there may be tears on the boy's cheek that the father traces on his son's face. All mean machismo vanishes, as it were, and all that is left is the pure, rarefied affection of a father for his youngest son—a son who carries his name. But since Yunior relates only this imagined version of this important moment in the family's history, the actual reunion may have been unremarkable.

When we examine the third story in this triad, "Fiesta, 1980," we immediately notice that Ramón and Yunior are at odds with one another. Yunior lives in fear of angering his father, and specifically, of vomiting in his new VW. Yunior is approximately twelve years old in this story—Ramón brought them to the United States in 1977, when Yunior was nine. The volatile relationship between father and son may also be a result of not knowing one another. In short, they are strangers to one another.

But as the title suggests, there is a party going on in the story. The celebration of Yunior's tía Yrma and tío Miguel's arrival to the United States is the impetus for this story, but it is mostly an occasion to explore the dynamic between Yunior and his father. Díaz depicts Ramón as an authoritarian with his defining characteristic of infidelity at the forefront. Rafa and Yunior's understanding that "Papi had been with that Puerto Rican woman he was seeing" (23) connects directly to Ramón's dealings in "Negocios." And though this is an important plot point in "Fiesta, 1980," the overarching concern of the story is Yunior's relationship with his father. The point of contention comes from Yunior's inability to ride in his father's Volkswagen van without throwing up. "I was never supposed to eat before our car trips," Yunior notes (26). When Ramón interrogates Yunior, pulling him to his feet by his ear, he menaces, "If you throw up——." Yunior's response to the pain is itself painful: "I won't, I cried, tears in my eyes, more out of reflex than pain." This type of father-son interaction is far from the idealized reunion Yunior imagined at the end of "Aguantando." He recalls the first time he vomited in his father's van, followed by Ramón's repeated cleaning of the messes. His father's "imaginative" punishments sting long after the fact: "He was pissed, though; he jammed his finger into my cheek, a nice solid thrust" (30). Unlike the tender moment in an imagined scenario where Ramón strokes his son's cheek, here the father subjects Yunior to a painful thrust to his cheek. Clearly Ramón is not the father Yunior so longed for as a child. The resulting disparity between the two scenarios would be devastating to any young boy.

Amid the party atmosphere of the story, there is feasting, dancing, and youthful debauchery, all of which Yunior observes, but he does not partake. His thoughts are of vomiting, leading his thoughts to the rides his father would take him on in the Volkswagen van. These were futile attempts to cure Yunior of his car sickness, mere excuses for Ramón to visit the Puerto Rican woman with whom he was having an affair. Though Ramón was cheating on his wife during the five years he was away from his family, Yunior was not aware of his father's inability to honor his wife at that time. But now, reunited as they are in the United States, Yunior not only can observe his father's disgraceful behavior firsthand, he has met his father's "sucia." What's more, she is nice to Yunior and calls him both "cute" and "the smart one" (36). Ramón is so untroubled by his affair that he thinks little of bringing his sons along with him on his assignations. The disparity in character between Yunior and his father is evident: Ramón indulges his urges at the cost of his wife's dignity, but Yunior must abstain from eating in the midst of a fiesta.

As the evening winds down, Yunior does take an indulgent moment in the form of a reverie concerning his mother. Like he once did with his father when he was away, Yunior remembers the one photograph of his mother before she met Ramón. It is a photograph of her in her youth, and Yunior thinks of her as "the woman my father met a year later on the Malecón, the woman Mami thought she'd always be" (41). Yunior stares at his mother as he recalls this precious image of her in the days before Ramón, and she smiles at him. "Suddenly I wanted to go over and hug her, for no other reason than I loved her, but there were about eleven fat jiggling bodies between us," Yunior says (41–42). Despite his devotion and love for his mother, he never tells her about the Puerto Rican woman. He's powerless to stop his father's cheating, and he is unable to tell his mother the truth of the situation. When he vomits time and again in his father's van, his untenable situation is made manifest. Natalie J. Friedman argues that the subject of adultery in "Fiesta, 1980" parallels "the experience of the immigrant narrative of Yunior's family and countless other Dominicans."[6] Indeed, Yunior's life is arguably shaped most potently by his immigrant experience and his observations of and participation in adulterous affairs of the men in his family. In "Fiesta, 1980," Yunior is sick from what he knows is happening but is powerless to stop. His father is a cheater, his brother has already begun to take after Ramón, and Yunior himself will most likely become the kind of man who has caused him so much anguish in his childhood.

"Negocios," "Aguantando," and "Fiesta, 1980" all trace the early formation of Yunior's sense of masculinity. Despite the rationale related for him in "Negocios," Ramón is quite unlikable in the earlier stories in which he appears, about the father-son relationship during Yunior's formative, prepubescent years both in the Dominican Republic and the United States. Certainly the sins of the father do not justify the kind of behavior Yunior revels in when we encounter him later in stories of his adulthood. However, these earlier stories provide the reader with an intriguing backstory to the formation of Yunior's sense of being a man. His father and his brother each serve as a kind of model for Yunior's later years. Even so, Yunior reveals his heightened emotionality that he often hides or reveals only to the reader of his stories—stories that he narrates many years after the fact. These stories are a testament to Yunior's saving grace—that he has found solace in the ability to weave certain traumatic events from his life into compelling stories. That he returns to narrate these stories is telling not as an attempt to garner sympathy or pity but rather as a sort of cathartic writing exercise that helps him comes to terms with his past. As we find out in later stories, Yunior, like his creator, has chosen the path of the writer.

"AURORA," "BOYFRIEND," "EDISON, NEW JERSEY," AND "HOW TO DATE A BROWNGIRL, BLACKGIRL, WHITEGIRL, OR HALFIE"

As a character Yunior often tells about his relationships with women, particularly as a means of self-exploration. Yunior comes to terms with his identity as a Dominican American man via his often misogynistic attitudes toward women, his inability to remain faithful to one woman at a time, and his missteps in love. Four stories in *Drown* reveal these nuances in the behavior of their Dominican American male protagonists: "Aurora," "Boyfriend," "Edison, New Jersey," and "How to Date a Browngirl, Blackgirl, Whitegirl, or Halfie."

To begin with, three of these stories never explicitly indicate that Yunior is the narrator; "How to Date" does mention Yunior, and its use of second-person narration makes it significant for other reasons. However, a similar narrator—a young, Dominican American man in the New Jersey/New York area, narrates the quartet of stories. There are notable markers that cohere to give the reader the impression that there is a high chance that it is Yunior, and when reading the quartet of stories as a unit, this cohesion comes to the fore. But in order to avoid confusion I will not refer to the at-times unnamed narrator as Yunior. My approach to these stories is that a given story need not explicitly announce the narrator's identity for it to be about Yunior.

If readers think of *Drown* as something like a composite novel or short-story cycle, then there is a thread that binds all of the stories into a whole. Indeed, there is no question that Yunior is the dominant element of the entire book.

These four stories have a Dominican male personality at their core. Each story also revels in the pleasures and pains associated with male-female relationships, and are about a Dominican man's experiences with love. Relationships are complex because people are complex. The narrators of the stories cannot comprehend the actions and motivations of women, though they make at least some attempt to understand. The narrators also reflect upon on their struggle to understand the nuances of love, sex, obsession, and desire—where the rational intellect meets the mystery of emotion. Finally, these stories all occur when the narrators are all young men, and the content of the stories reflects that.

"Aurora" is the first story in *Drown* that takes on the perspective of a young man, and is the third story in the book. Lucero, the narrator, is in his late teens or early twenties. The story's title refers to Lucero's sometime girlfriend, a young woman whom the narrator describes as skinny, drug using, and recently released from juvenile detention. She is not the first woman with whom Lucero has had a relationship, but she does appear to be the first that has crossed over into what we would characterize as a love interest. Does Lucero love Aurora? Does she love him? The story is notable for initiating the reader into Díaz's fondness for exactly this sort of plot, one in which the narrator dissects his relationship with a previous lover.

The major character in "Aurora" besides the title character and Lucero is Cut, the narrator's close friend, roommate, and drug business partner. The story opens with a drug buy involving the narrator and Cut, as they smoke marijuana and parse their inventory for sale, all the while with Aurora on the narrator's mind. It is important to trace these two issues (drug use and love) within the story because one illuminates the other. Lucero, a drug dealer who feeds the addictions of others, is himself addicted to Aurora. Despite Cut's warnings and admonitions, Lucero can't leave her.

Lucero expects Aurora to come by because it is Friday, and Fridays are the days she can expect Lucero and Cut to have drugs on hand. Already the complication of the story is established—is it love that unites these two, or is it the drugs? Their encounters are passionate and, quite often, violent. Cut, so stoned at the story's opening that he thought he was drooling all over his face, gives Lucero sensible advice when Aurora shows up: "Don't do it. . . . Just leave it alone" (48). Lucero reveals Cut's ambivalence regarding Aurora, saying, "He's not a fan of Aurora, never gives me the messages she leaves with him." Despite Cut's shortcomings, he seems to offer Lucero practical counsel. Of course, if he is indeed "addicted to" Aurora, no amount of reasoned argument is going to make a difference. As a drug dealer, Lucero knows this better than anyone. He cannot help but give in to his feelings of affection for Aurora time and again.

That the drug business and Lucero's love for Aurora are part and parcel of each other is evident in the juxtaposition of the story's structure. The section "A Working Day" details a typical day of dealing to "a lot of kids and some older folks who haven't had a job or a haircut since the last census" (51), and precedes the section titled "One of Our Nights." The latter is a portrait that is on one hand tender and affectionate, and on the other paranoid and violent. Interestingly, it is in this section where one of Lucero's physical traits is underscored: "You got those long eyelashes that make me want to cry, she says. How could anybody hurt a man with eyelashes like this?" (52). In a later story, "Edison, New Jersey," the unnamed narrator's eyelashes will also be referenced. While it seems a minor detail, it helps us connect some of the stories that do not explicitly identify the narrator.

In "Aurora" we determine the narrator's identity in the section titled "Lucero." Aurora seems to confess an abortion she has had: "I would have named it after you, she said. . . . You're named after a star" (59). Lucero admits that he wasn't aware of the child, and their inability to communicate reveals the emotional distance between the two despite their physical proximity. When Aurora states, "You're named after a star," ostensibly she's referring to the *lucero del alba*, what some varieties of Spanish name the morning star. In Latin, *aurora* means "dawn," and so we have two characters named, ironically, after bright celestial phenomena that connote the start of a new day. Aurora will ultimately return to juvie, and Cut views this as an opportunity for Lucero to break from her once and for all. But Lucero cannot.

The final section depicts the love and violence that characterizes their relationship, and the story ends, "She ran her nails over my side. A week from then she would be asking me again, begging actually, telling me all the good things we'd do and after a while I hit her and made the blood come out of her ear like a worm but right then, in that apartment, we seemed like we were normal folks. Like maybe everything was fine" (65). The reality is that everything is not fine. Cut is correct in his assessment of Lucero and Aurora's relationship. The two are star-crossed, caught between a fantasy life and a violent reality. Aurora's temporary imaginings of a life with Lucero are as fleeting as a hit from a joint, and the crash that follows is as heavy as Lucero's fist to the side of Aurora's head.

"Aurora" brings several salient issues in Díaz's writing to the surface. Though Yunior does not narrate this story, the masculine codes of drug culture makes Lucero similar to Yunior in many ways. Both narrators publicly use a fierce bravado akin to "the dozens," an insult-laden form of wordplay predominantly used in some African American male cultures.[7] In private, however, the narrators also use more sentimental language indicative of a romantic sensibility. Yunior's stories of childhood especially reveal the heightened emotional language related to his experiences. Similar instances of tenderness appear in Lucero's narration, such as when he admits, "You know how it is when you get back with somebody you've loved. It felt better than it ever was, better than it ever could be again" (64). But Lucero is also prone to violence, as evident in the many times he admits to wanting to punch Aurora until she's bloody. Such direct expressions of domestic violence rarely appear in stories Yunior narrates.

From a formal perspective, "Aurora" takes a troubled woman's story as its subject but relates it from a man's point of observation. Though the reader learns about Lucero's small-time drug business, the protagonist remains transfixed on Aurora. Lucero has concern for Aurora, and if he were another person he might have the wherewithal to help her. But he is only slightly less damaged than Aurora, and so the pain he feels for her is amplified because he operates under the code of self-preservation as well as hypermasculinity. Lucero is willing to sell drugs to kids, but he recognizes Aurora's plight as tragic. One section title proclaims "I could save you," but it's only so much bullshit, as Cut recognizes. Lucero cannot even save himself—from his drug business, from his violent tendencies, from Aurora. The light from their ironic names is destined to burn brightly yet quickly.

But who will help Aurora? From Lucero's perspective, no one wants to help her. Does empathy drive Lucero's interest in Aurora, or is it that he has misinterpreted empathy for love? A drug dealer would know the effects of the substances he deals; metaphorically Lucero is killing Aurora while he abuses her with physical violence. The story is steeped in irony: a drug dealer who wants to save his drug-addicted girlfriend that he occasionally beats up. Aurora's story is tragic, and one cannot help but consider the unspoken backstory that led her to the place in which we find her in the story that bears her name. There is an elegiac undertone to the story, and it follows Díaz's use of a narrator who effectively memorializes a friend or girlfriend by telling a story of lost love or friendship. This technique affords Díaz the opportunity of telling two stories at once—the story of the narrator and the story of the narrator's subject.

Díaz continues with this technique in the near-vignette-length story, the shortest story in the entire book, "Boyfriend." The story features another unnamed narrator who belongs to the cadre of Dominican male narrators Díaz often employs. "Boyfriend" is a natural follow-up to "Aurora," and the opening sentence connects the two stories: "I should have been careful with the weed" (111). Like Lucero in "Aurora," the narrator of "Boyfriend" uses narcotics, and it affects his sleep. Alone and unable to sleep, he listens to the couple in the apartment directly above him as they vacillate between argument and lovemaking, reminiscent of Lucero and Aurora's relationship. The narrator designates the couple as "Boyfriend" and "Girlfriend," introducing them by reporting how their argument began. He makes the point of noting that Boyfriend wants space: "I knew Boyfriend a little. I saw him at the bars and saw some of the girls he used to bring home while she was away. He just needed more space to cheat" (111). The recurring topic of infidelity is once more at the center of a Díaz story.

As we should come to expect, when Díaz-created male narrators tell a story about someone else, it is usually a means of exploring their own foibles and character flaws; they cannot confront these shortcomings directly. "They sounded a lot like me and my old girlfriend Loretta, but I swore to myself that I would stop thinking about her ass, even though every Cleopatra-looking Latina in the city made me stop and wish she would come back to me," the narrator confesses (111). In this case, the arguing couple upstairs triggers the narrator to reveal his relationship issues with his ex-girlfriend. Listening to Boyfriend and Girlfriend fight overhead is like listening to himself fight with Loretta, like the fights between Lucero and Aurora. Despite his refusal to be affected by the arguing upstairs, the narrator can't help but take it personally: "It would have broken my heart if it hadn't been so damn familiar. I guess I'd gotten numb to that sort of thing. I had heart-leather like walruses got blubber" (112).

In many ways, the couple upstairs is like a better version of the narrator and Loretta: "Hell, they both could have been models, which was what they probably were . . . . People like these were untouchables to me, raised on some other planet and then transplanted into my general vicinity to remind me how bad I was living" (112). Though it may be that the narrator has well-developed heart-leather, his thoughts consistently turn to Loretta. Does the narrator have a sort of inferiority complex with the couple that is literally and figuratively above him? To a certain extent he does, or he wouldn't point to the deficiencies in his relationship with his ex. On the other hand, Boyfriend and Girlfriend, with their model looks and well-honed communication skills, also end up with a wrecked relationship. Problems of the heart can affect anyone, anywhere.

The story turns when Boyfriend stops coming to see Girlfriend. When enough time has passed, the narrator musters enough courage to invite her over for coffee. He plays Andrés Jiménez, drinks El Pico coffee, and proceeds to have nothing to say. For someone so good at storytelling and narrating, he is deficient in the art of conversation. To make matters worse, the narrator experiences the worst gas of his life and has to excuse himself several times. He ought to feel excited, invigorated by having such a beautiful woman as Girlfriend in his apartment. Instead, he can only note how much "shabbier" having her there makes him feel (116). Putting two melancholic people together in a room doesn't make it a fiesta, Díaz seems to be saying.

By the end of the story, Girlfriend has cut her hair and the narrator tells her, "Makes you look fierce" (117). Perhaps Girlfriend has moved on with her life, but the narrator remains alone, even if temporarily. The story's title, "Boyfriend," is indicative not only of the guy upstairs but of the narrator's former life as Loretta's boyfriend. He never reveals why Loretta and he are no longer together, but her memory persists, along with the hurt of her absence. One day she said, "I like him. He's a hard worker," and suddenly Loretta wanted out of the relationship (114). Since cheating is often a struggle for the male characters in Díaz's fiction, we are left to wonder if the narrator cheated on Loretta. In "Boyfriend," as in the story that follows, the protagonists, freed from the expectations of a relationship, have every opportunity to sleep with a woman who is not their former girlfriend. Still, each decides against it. "Boyfriend" displays Díaz's technique of having a narrator tell someone else's story while simultaneously telling his own.

"Edison, New Jersey" employs this technique as well, amplified through the use of several characters. The unnamed narrator, who at the very least happens to have the same exquisite eyelashes as Lucero, here appears not as a drug dealer but as an employee of a company that deals with billiard tables, card tables, and slot machines. This narrator performs the backbreaking yeoman's work of moving and delivering pool tables, and once more we see Díaz bringing together issues of bodily abuse with matters of the heart. In addition, Díaz designs the story with multiple problematic relationships that provide the impetus for the narrative. The narrator often reflects on his recent relationship with a woman he only calls "the girlfriend." It is an ironic moniker because the girlfriend is clearly no longer *his* girlfriend and hearkens back to the story "Boyfriend." Wayne, the narrator's delivery partner, is cheating on his wife with a woman named Charlene, and Wayne tells the narrator about his extramarital affairs. But central to the story is the narrator's encounter with a Dominican woman who remains nameless. The Dominican woman lives with a man named Pruitt, who has purchased a billiard table that the narrator and Wayne try to deliver several times. The various relationships all allow the narrator an opportunity to ruminate on his failed relationship with the girlfriend.

The narrator performs backbreaking work and often skims the till at the company whenever he can. "Since I'm no good at cleaning or selling slot machines," he narrates, "I slouch behind the front register and steal. I don't ring anything up, and pocket what comes in. . . . A hundred-buck haul's not unusual for me and back in the day, when the girlfriend used to pick me up, I'd buy her anything she wanted, dresses, silver rings, lingerie. Sometimes I blew it all on her" (125). Because he spends it all on the girlfriend, there is the sense that the narrator cannot afford to keep her. The lack and abundance of money is a salient issue in "Edison, New Jersey." The narrator steals so he can buy the girlfriend material things, yet Pruitt, the customer who has more money than he knows what to do with, seemingly cares little for his live-in Dominican girlfriend. The various incongruities among the many relationships frustrate the narrator while also allowing him to reflect on his damaged relationship.

As we have already seen in many of Díaz's stories, infidelity is of central concern in this story. The narrator does not admit to having cheated on his girlfriend, yet the reader is left to wonder why his girlfriend has in effect left him, for a guy named Dan. In the tiny vignettes the narrator relates from a time when he and his girlfriend were together, there are expressions of love and passion. He only hints at what caused the trouble in their relationship: "We stopped playing only when it started to go wrong for us, when I'd wake up and listen to the traffic outside without waking her, when everything was a fight" (132). It is plausible that the girlfriend caught the narrator being unfaithful based on his disdain for Wayne's infidelity and the decision not to have sex with Pruitt's girlfriend, each of which reflects the narrator's regret at his actions.

When infidelity is a significant issue in any of Díaz's stories, one feels that the unfaithful narrator may learn his lesson, or that he may come through the experience better for the heartbreak. One of the reasons that this is even possible is that the narrators are often so painfully honest in plainly stating their flaws. It is certainly hard to root for a cheater, but it is also difficult to root against these cheating narrators. In "Edison, New Jersey," as in "Aurora," the narrator seemingly wants to save a young woman from her environment. Aurora is having unprotected sex, and the bruises on her body along with her shocking weight loss hint that she has contracted a grave disease such as HIV, and Lucero recognizes the seriousness of her situation. But Lucero may be as flawed as Aurora, and thus any real intentions he ultimately might have come to nothing. The narrator in "Edison" might be seen as an improvement over Lucero because he takes a risk in trying to help Pruitt's girlfriend. He certainly doesn't have to help her, and Wayne advises him to leave it alone: "You can't do it" (135). But the narrator uses Wayne's infidelity against him, "You tagged Charlene, didn't you?" he asks. "Sure did," Wayne responds. The narrator, who wants to get Pruitt's girlfriend out of a potentially dangerous, if not exploitative situation, uses Wayne's rationalization of cheating as a justification for getting her out of Pruitt's house. What Wayne doesn't know, what he could never imagine, is that the narrator doesn't have sex in mind.

It is a small victory for the narrator. Later on, purely out of curiosity, he calls Pruitt's house on several occasions until the Dominican woman answers. He tells Wayne, who says, "Pretty predictable. She's probably in love with the guy. You know how it is" (139). The narrator admits, "I sure do." Indeed, he does know how it is. He knows the difficulty in letting go of the one you love. In making the attempt to help the woman, the narrator has helped himself and perhaps has proven that he can be the kind of man the girlfriend wanted all along. Despite his mother and sister's prayer that he and the girlfriend will reunite, there are never such reunions in Díaz's fiction. Even Yunior's father, who rejoins his family after years of separation, can never fully remain faithful to his wife. Whereas Ramón can never break his cycle of infidelity, the cohort of young, male, Dominican narrators that populate Díaz's fiction fall and try again. What keeps them from being despicable human beings is their capacity to recognize and embrace the emotional turmoil that results when they have been unfaithful.

On the other hand, Díaz's stories make a strong case for infidelity as being the default setting for the Dominican man, as it were. An unfaithful Dominican man is so ordinary as to be expected in Díaz's fiction. That Díaz's narrators recognize their infidelity as the source of their heartbreak speaks to a generational divide, as well as a cultural divide. The migration from the Dominican Republic to the United States motivates this as well, along with the conflation of a Dominican man's sense of identity with the sexual act. *The Brief Wondrous Life of Oscar Wao* is a novel that, at least in part, concerns a Dominican man's fear of dying a virgin.

Before there was an Oscar Wao, there was "How to Date a Browngirl, Blackgirl, Whitegirl, or Halfie," a step-by-step guide to getting laid. The story is without question one of the most anthologized of the stories in *Drown*, in part because it handles so many issues related to identity and masculinity as well as because of its use of second-person narration. Like "Boyfriend," it is one of the shorter stories in the collection, and it is the only story of the quartet examined in this section that explicitly invokes Yunior by name. In one respect, "How to Date" is told in a how-to style. However, because of the second-person narration, Yunior is both the narrator and the narratee, as Daniel Bautista has argued.[8] In other words, the story is a bit like Yunior telling himself how he should handle a date with a variety of women, depending on race, ethnicity, language, and class. There is a flowchart sensibility to the story in that individual decisions yield particular outcomes. For example, if the "girl is from around the way, take her to El Cibao for dinner. . . . If she's not from around the way, Wendy's will do" (145). If the date is X type of woman, do Y action, and so on.

Second-person narration, potentially clumsy in the hands of other writers, almost gives off sparks in Díaz's hands. It is quite easy to imagine most of his first-person narrators speaking, for they emulate an actual speaker's free-flowing ability to riff, joke, and get serious from one moment to the next. But unlike many second-person narrators who address a narratee whose identity a reader can temporarily adopt, it's quite clear that Yunior's narratee is himself. It begs the question: why would a narrator tell himself a story? One must consider that the story, delivered in the second-person address, is hypothetical. According to Marisel Moreno: "With each successive step or situation, the reader learns more about Yunior, the narrator, since his step-by-step advice appears to mirror his own experiences. Through this narrative technique, the boundaries between the 'real' and the hypothetical, and those of the past and the present, are equally blurred since it is not clear whether Yunior's narrative constitutes a rearticulation of his lived experience or is simply a product of his imagination."[9] The story is not one person speaking to another. This point may seem minor, but it has significant ramifications if it is the case. It doesn't seem hypothetical because so many of the events in the story are distinct. For instance, consider the moment the narrator invokes Yunior's name. The narrator states: "Hope that you don't run into your nemesis, Howie, the Puerto Rican kid with the two killer mutts. He walks them all over the neighborhood and every now and then the mutts corner themselves a cat and tear it to shreds, Howie laughing as the cat flips up in the air, its neck twisted around like an owl, red meat showing through the fur. If his dogs haven't cornered a cat, he will walk behind you and ask, Hey, Yunior, is that your new fuckbuddy?" (146). Díaz tends to feature narrators that write about someone else while at the same time using that story to reflect the narrators' experience and identity. Here he has Yunior as both narrating subject *and* narrator. In other words, Yunior learns about himself by telling himself a story.

If we accept the premise that Yunior is both the narrator and the narratee, it elevates the emotional poignancy of the story for several reasons. First, Yunior gives directions that emphasize a fluidity of self determined by the identity position of his date. Second, because he understands that identity has to remain flexible, he suppresses fixed identity markers such as photographs, Afro hairdos, dark skin, "busted up Spanish," and even his handwriting. When he states, "Tell her that you love her hair, that you love her skin, her lips, because, in truth, you love them more than you love your own," the truth is that Yunior could easily be chastising himself (147).

There is not irrefutable evidence that Yunior is narrating. However, the design of the story, along with what we know of Yunior in other stories, all seem to point to the possibility that Yunior is exploring how to navigate the dizzying business of love for a Dominican man. The narrator in "Boyfriend" remarks, "I used to think those were the barrio rules, Latinos and blacks in, whites out—a place we down cats weren't supposed to go. But love teaches you. Clears your head of any rules" (114). The narrator in "How to Date" understands full well that love demands one follow very specific rules. There are rules of economics, just as the narrator of "Edison, New Jersey" discovers. There are rules regarding fidelity. And there are rules according to racial, ethnic, cultural, and linguistic norms that comprise all possible permutations of pairings for Yunior.

Yunior is a young man who must perform his identity. The girl he is with and the expectations she carries with her dictate who he is and how he sees himself. On the surface, we might expect that Yunior is chameleon-like because he will do whatever he must in order to have sex with his dates. However, Yunior is sensitive and often emotionally vulnerable. He cannot just embrace who he is and be who he wants to be. Instead, he must fake an identity so as not to have his date reject him. The fear of rejection is the story's prime mover.

Indeed, in this quartet of stories each protagonist is incapable of doing what his heart desires. By nature, each has a caring spirit and is emotionally moved to connect with a woman in a way that the macho scripts of Dominican men do not allow. If we are gauging these young men solely based on their actions, we are doing the stories a disservice. Díaz allows the narrators the freedom to explore the many constraints on Dominican male identity and how his characters negotiate those constraints, however imperfectly. The good that these young men would do, the heartfelt compassion they might feel for a woman, is tossed aside in favor of macho personas that mask what they feel. The how-to nature of "How to Date" becomes less of a user's manual or set of directions and more of a series of cultural scripts that someone like Yunior is compelled to follow. Ironically, despite the "how-to" nature of the story, the situations dictate Yunior's actions and not the reverse. Díaz is careful not to exonerate his male characters from the consequences of their often boneheaded choices. But he does lend a bit of nuance to the larger forces that are at work in a Dominican man's life.

"DROWN"

The title story of the collection is unique among the rest for several reasons. First, it holds a privileged position in sharing its title with the book. Second, it is the only story that explicitly takes up the issue of male homosexuality with equal measures of distance and affection. Third, "Drown" doesn't appear to be within Yunior's life experience. Nor does it feature a narrator who weighs his own efforts at relationships with women against the subjects of his narration such as Girlfriend or Pruitt's live-in girlfriend. The only overt connection to any of the other stories is the mention of the drug-dealing Lucero, who sells to the "crackheads" (93). Finally, as an indication of its importance and "position of privilege," the story is centrally located in the book, appearing as the fifth story out of ten.[10]

"Drown" rests on the fault line where male bonding and male homosexual desire meet. The narrator, an unnamed Dominican boy one year from graduating high school, concentrates on the ebb and flow of his relationship with his friend, Beto. Though the tense occasionally shifts thanks to the use of flashback, it is mostly narrated in the present. But time has proven to be of central concern to the narrator. He is fast approaching an age where he must decide whether he will stay or leave home, and, generally speaking, what he will do with his life after he graduates from high school. Like Yunior, the narrator doesn't let on that he is a voracious reader and that he is exceptionally literate. When he has to explain to Beto what "no expectorating" means on the sign at the swimming pool, his friend is astonished: "Shit, he said. Where did you learn that?" (94). When the narrator demurs, Beto insists. It is a crucial moment in the story that provides the impetus for the title itself: "Tell me. He hated when I knew something he didn't. He put his hands on my shoulders and pushed me under. He was wearing a cross and cutoff jeans. He was stronger than me and

held me down until water flooded my nose and throat. Even then I
didn't tell him; he thought I didn't read, not even dictionaries" (94).

When the story begins, Beto and the narrator already find themselves distanced in their relationship. Beto has been away for a short
while, apparently to college or university, and has now returned. The
narrator's mother wonders why her son isn't excited to see Beto. The
narrator reveals that Beto is now out as a "pato," slang for gay, but that
"two years ago we were friends and he would walk into the apartment
without knocking, his heavy voice rousing my mother from the Spanish of her room and drawing me up from the basement, a voice that
crackled and made you think of uncles or grandfathers" (91). Not only
were the two boys close, Beto is slightly older than the narrator; there
is something to him, a kind of charisma that the narrator admires. It
is a relationship that echoes Yunior's consistent deference to his older
brother Rafa.

Further, Beto cannot stand his neighborhood. Knowing that he
will leave for college soon, he is beside himself with the thought of
leaving. Meanwhile, the narrator confesses that he has no options
once he graduates from high school. It is this sense of being trapped,
this feeling of overwhelming claustrophobia that also pings back to
the story's title. During the day the "heat in the apartments was like
something heavy that had come inside to die," and at night the two
often jump the fence of the community pool, where they "were never
alone, every kid with legs was there" (92). With so many children
in the dark and the sheer risk of them drowning, the danger of the
unguarded pool speaks to the possibility of a threat in all aspects of
the narrator's life.

Indeed, dangers lurk everywhere. The narrator's mother speaks of
a recently assaulted woman named Lorena, perhaps another apartment tenant. Later, the narrator reminisces on the outrageous acts
of theft he and Beto had committed before their friendship soured.
From this violence, we see another act of tenderness between the boys
when Beto holds the narrator's hand lovingly when they are caught

stealing. The bond between them grows amid the violence and looming threats.

Díaz skillfully uses narrative time in "Drown." From section to section he juxtaposes the narrator of the present—the narrator who has cut himself off from his best friend when he discovers his friend is gay—to the younger version of the narrator *before* he and Beto become sexual partners. The narrator muses how he "and the boys drive to New Brunswick" to drink and hit the bars and clubs and "stare at the college girls" (102). On the way home, they drive by "the fag bar, which never seems to close. Patos are all over the parking lot, drinking and talking" (103). One of the narrator's "boys," Alex, at times will stop at the gay bar directly to torment and terrorize the clientele just for laughs.

Near the end of the story, the narrator takes us to those moments that end his relationship with Beto. "Twice. That's it," he proclaims at the opening of the section, dismissing his participation as an anomaly. While watching some of Beto's father's porn, Beto reaches into the narrator's shorts and begins to masturbate him. After he has an orgasm, the narrator leaves as if nothing had happened. The next day he decides to distance himself from Beto, "terrified that I would end up abnormal, a fucking pato, but he was my best friend and back then that mattered to me more than anything" (104). That night, they both end up at the community pool, and from there, to his parent's apartment. They are the only ones there for hours. In only their towels, Beto initiates their sexual contact and even tells the narrator that he'll "stop if he wants" (105). But the narrator in his sexual bliss recalls a teacher who once compared his students to the space shuttles. "A few of you are going to make it. Those are the orbiters. But the majority of you are just going to burn out. Going nowhere" (106). In the middle of this memory, the sound of the hallway door opening startles the narrator to his senses. While Beto laughs, the narrator says, "Fuck this."

The story ends with the narrator thinking of Beto, remembering that Beto had given him a book on the day he left for college. The book forever remains a mystery; the narrator throws it away without ever looking at it. As he sits next to his mother on the couch as they watch television together, Beto's words ring in his mind: "You can't be anywhere forever" (107). Though his father left him years before, a fact that he deeply resents, the narrator now understands that it may be time for him to leave home and see what the world has to offer him. Even if it means leaving his mother for whom he cares so deeply. He knows there is more to life than selling low-grade dope to the neighborhood kids.

There is a bittersweet acknowledgment of what love is and how true love can drown a person as the story closes. Dorothy Stringer, however, reads "Drown" in light of its "own homophobia, attenuated and self-interrogating but not yet annihilated. . . . Moreover, it sets aside virtually all the material facts of gay life . . . we do not see a man love another man, despite the fact that that love happens every day, in every kind of place, including deindustrialized mid-New Jersey immigrant neighborhoods."[11] Cultural codes and vigorous antigay sentiment drown the close friendship and perhaps love that Beto and the narrator shared. The sexual exploration of these two teens, even if the narrator ultimately did not wish to pursue it, should not have ended the close friendship he had with Beto. "Drown," as in other stories in the collection, reveals the pressures that motivate men— and especially Latino men—to act irrationally in matters of love and affection. It highlights the kind of situations in which a man resorts to scripted "how-to" instructions to guide him rather than allowing his emotions dictate his actions. The male narrators of the collection cannot pursue relationships *on their terms* rather than society's terms. Yunior might potentially have a friendship with Ysrael, and he realizes this right at the moment Rafa shatters a Coke bottle against Ysrael's head. Yunior might love his father, and his father might love him if they could only understand each other and recapture the missing time they lost during their years of separation. "I could save you," Lucero thinks as he watches Aurora enter a crack house, but he can't rise above the machismo codes long enough to help her; he can't even save himself. And even when a narrator does take a risk and steps outside of his prescribed role, such as the narrator in "Edison, New Jersey," his actions are negated when the girl ultimately returns to Pruitt's house. Whether it is a failing of character or an inability to break through the expectations of community, these narrators are unable to find what they most desire: a substantive, lasting, meaningful relationship with the ones they love.

CHAPTER 2

The Brief Wondrous Life of Oscar Wao (2007)

D íaz's first novel dispelled any doubts that its author was a writer of merit, if not a literary sensation. *Drown* had met with the kind of critical praise first story collections rarely enjoy, and many critics wondered if Díaz could follow up vigorously with a second book. Though he was writing manuscripts, his second book would not be published for another decade. *The Brief Wondrous Life of Oscar Wao* would go on to garner numerous nominations for prestigious literary awards and win the Pulitzer Prize for Fiction in 2008 as well as the National Book Critics Circle Award in the same year.

As a result of both the novel's high acclaim and its striking narrative content and structure, the majority of scholarly examinations of Díaz's works have concentrated on this book, which Ramón Saldívar persuasively argues is an example of "'historical fantasy' and 'speculative realism'" and features a story structure that is an "odd amalgam of historical novel, bildungsroman, postmagical realism, sci-fi, fantasy, and super-hero comic romance."[1] Scholarship on the novel has investigated a number of critical aspects regarding its use of history, structure, and comic books. For instance, Monica Hanna describes the interweaving of genres as a means by which Díaz's book aims for "resistance history," the result of which she calls a "historiographic battle royal" between historical events and the narrator's (and the reader's) attempt to reconstruct history, making *Oscar Wao*, in Hanna's estimation, a clear example of Linda Hutcheon's concept of historiographic metafiction.[2] Indeed, it often does appear that Díaz's project is to void a biased historical record while simultaneously supplanting it with his own. Daniel Bautista has investigated Díaz's use of what Bautista terms "comic book realism"—an irreverent mix of realism and popular culture—as a principally salient feature of the novel.[3] In a similar vein, Anne Garland Mahler makes the important argument that in Yunior, Díaz has constructed a superhero "who creates the zafa—or counterspell—to the evil forces of the fukú, as a writer who uses the pen to shed light on the existence of the violent structures of power that have been concealed . . . that Díaz promotes a writing that does not repress its own inherent violence but rather exposes it in order to disarm tyrannical power of perhaps its most effective weapon: the written word."[4] In addition to these perspectives, not only is the importance of the transnational evident in the geographic spaces of New Jersey and the Dominican Republic but Africa, as a historical umbilicus, plays a significant role in *Oscar Wao*.

Díaz devises an impetus for the narrative progression that comes out of Africa. Díaz locates his metonym for Africa in what Dominicans call *fukú*, a curse of the highest order that, by and large, has its origins in that continent. Not only does Yunior hold the dictator Trujillo responsible for the specific familial *fukú* that dominates Oscar's story, on the opening page of *Oscar Wao* he metonymically tethers Africa to what would later become the Dominican Republic: "They say it came first from Africa, carried in the screams of the enslaved; that it was the death bane of the Tainos, uttered just as one world perished and another began; that it was a demon drawn into Creation through the nightmare door that was cracked open in the Antilles."[5]

The opening salvo exemplifies Díaz's direct, frank manner, one that already establishes the speculative-generic tone of the novel. In a story ostensibly about Dominicans and their history, the seventh word is "Africa," the fourteenth is "enslaved." It is clear that *Oscar*

Wao is as much about inscribing the blank page where Africa and the legacy of slavery ought to be as it is about the Dominican Republic—or the United States, for that matter. The fukú curse is a type of original sin of the New World that derives its power from the outrage of slavery, and fukú drives the novel to its bittersweet end. Curses are usually engendered by a transgression and function as a means of retribution, if not atonement. Fukú originates from a Eurocentrism that has historically disregarded Africa as an equal in the Dominican Republic and has sought to obliterate all vestiges of Africa throughout the society, as José David Saldívar claims:

> Yunior's theorizing of the *fukú americanus* in his novel's prologue
> allows his readers to comprehend the constitutive relationship
> between the historical a priori of Eurocentric genocide and its
> hegemonic history of off-shore activities. His remarkable framing of
> the *fukú americanus* as an alternative unit of analysis beyond the unit
> of the nation-state further allows him to think through the US and
> Eurocentric structures of hegemonic thought and representation that
> continue to dominate the globe today. It signals, too, the planetary
> networks within which fukú Americanity, globalization (capitalism),
> and modernity themselves all became possible.[6]

Yunior proclaims in footnote twenty-nine, "The Europeans were the original fukú, no stopping them" (244). In a larger sense, then, this curse may be a part of present-day Dominicans who also disregard their Africanness in favor of a European ancestry.

As an intertext, the fukú legend is strictly a matter of folklore and hearsay—an oral story that is passed down from generation to generation. It does not concern Yunior that the fukú curse is not a matter of verifiable fact, though he does make an attempt to provide the proof in the novel's prologue:

> You want a final conclusive answer to the Warren Commission's
> question, Who killed JFK? Let me, your humble Watcher, reveal

once and for all the God's Honest Truth: It wasn't the mob or LBJ
or the ghost of Marilyn Fucking Monroe. It wasn't aliens or the
KGB or a lone gunman. It wasn't the Hunt Brothers of Texas or Lee
Harvey or the Trilateral Commission. It was Trujillo; it was the fukú.
Where in coñazo do you think the so-called Curse of the Kennedys
comes from? How about Vietnam? Why do you think the greatest
power in the world lost its first war to a Third World country like
Vietnam? I mean, Negro, *please*. (4)

Of course, speculation provides so much of the foundation of Yunior's
narrative that it makes sense that he can give only speculative evidence of the fukú curse. He bases so much of the unexplainable
aspects of his narrative on fukú that the curse, and Yunior's belief in
it, suffuse every aspect of Oscar's story. In other words, Yunior cannot begin to narrate Oscar's story without this important intertextual,
folkloric belief. It is not enough for him to dredge up the forgotten
moments in Dominican history in "historiographic battle royal," as
Hanna argues. Because belief in the fukú is a matter of faith and at
least a modicum of speculation, Yunior consistently calls upon two
exemplars of speculative literature to aid his narrative worldmaking:
The Fantastic Four and *The Lord of the Rings*.

All of these takes on Díaz's narrative style help clarify the rich-
ness and complexity of his novel. However, Díaz's contribution of
a virtuosic narrative worldmaker to American letters is a singular accomplishment. Yunior is a linguistically unrestrained narrator
who unabashedly explores a myriad of topics, such as the African
ancestry of his panoply of characters; the invocation of science fiction, fantasy, and comic book; intertexts as a crucial narrative feature;
the ever-present threat of being expunged from the historical record;
and much more. My examination of *Oscar Wao* takes up many of the
salient issues surrounding the novel, beginning first and foremost
with the title character, followed by an analysis of what is by now a
familiar feature of Díaz's fiction, his narrator. I will also highlight sev-

eral meaningful issues that the novel raises, including its engagement with African ancestry, the role of women, its intertextual interplay, and its uses of speculative genres.

GHETTO NERD AT THE CENTER OF THE NOVEL

While Díaz often employs character narrators that narrate the stories of other characters, none have given as many words to his subject as Yunior does Oscar de León, the ill-fated Dominican American kid whose story dominates much of the novel. Oscar is unlike any character in all of Latino literature. He is not a streetwise, sexual urbanite like the narrator from John Rechy's *City of Night* nor a wide-eyed innocent boy like the narrator of Rudolfo Anaya's *Bless Me, Ultima*. He is not the child of Tomás Rivera's *y no se lo tragó la tierra*, hard working as he slowly but determinedly comes of age. And Oscar is certainly not one of Hijuelos's Mambo Kings.

That is not to say that Oscar does not confront similar hardships and frustrations as these other characters of precedent. Like Rivera's protagonist, Oscar finds himself between two cultures, as well as being caught in a persistent cycle of migration. Like the Mambo Kings, as improbable as it may at first seem, Oscar is smitten by American culture. For Cesar and Nestor Castillo, the troubled brothers at the heart of Hijuelos's Pulitzer Prize–winning novel, the allure of American television via *I Love Lucy* and the enchantment of the live music scene both motivates and complicates their efforts to become successful in America. And like the narrator from *Bless Me, Ultima*, Oscar does have an idealistic view of the world—one that is not simply explained away by his youth.

Despite his similarities to other Latino fictional characters, however, I maintain that he is *unlike* any that have come before. Ironically, what makes Oscar such a unique Latino character—what pushes him from conventionality and expected tropes is what would make him a stereotype in other sorts of fiction. If we could remove certain markers of his Latinidad from the storyworld he inhabits, Oscar would become recognizable to readers as a stereotypical nerd figure. He's overweight, has an extensive vocabulary, is mocked by his peers, perseverates on science fiction and fantasy, is an aspiring writer of genre fiction, and is unpopular with women. The key difference is that we have not seen this sort of nerd figure, at least, not to the level of prominence Oscar occupies in Díaz's novel, in any notable work of Latino/a literature.

Surely this is a turn in the development of Latino/a literature—to have the title character of a Latino/a novel that resists readers' conventional understandings of what Latinos look like, of what they sound like, of the types of music they listen to, what kinds of movies they watch, and so forth. Remove Oscar's Latinidad and he is exactly the sort of character that drives those films from the 1980s like *Weird Science*, *Can't Buy Me Love*, or *Revenge of the Nerds* that helped solidify the nerd stereotype.[7] Relevant to my discussion here is that the nerd figure will endure bullying with grace, bear ridicule with aplomb, and accept the social hierarchy with requisite meekness. But what he (it is almost always a "he") longs for most of all, and what will motivate him to throw off the shackles of nerdiness is the promise of female companionship. Oscar may be a new addition to a long list of nerds in American literature, but he is the first Latino nerd.

Indeed, *The Brief Wondrous Life of Oscar Wao* is so wonderfully unconventional precisely because its title character has no equivalent in the history of Latino/a literature. At the level of form, Díaz blends genres and tropes to yield new combinations. But Oscar's arrival is not anomalous. That is to say, if Oscar is a nerd—a fanboy of the highest order—then he has company in the novel's narrator, Yunior, and the novel's author, Díaz himself. What is it about Oscar, "Latino, obese, sensitive, needy, a comic-book geek, an intellectual, and a would-be lover"[8] that makes him such an important figure?

In fact, this last question can be thought of as the impetus for the novel outright. From within the storyworld, readers and critics may question why someone like Yunior, who, from the other stories in which he figures in some important way, is on the surface nothing like Oscar, would go to the trouble to write an entire book about him. Whereas Oscar fears that he may be the only man of Dominican ancestry to die a virgin, Yunior cannot stop narrating his tumultuous affairs and sexual conquests. Or, when he's not discussing his experiences with love and sex, Yunior is telling those stories of his brother, Rafa, or of his father, Ramón. With the exception of the stories that deal with Ysrael in *Drown*, Yunior does not tell stories about other characters unless they are men who are related to him or women that he wants to have (or is having) a sexual relationship with. Therefore, that he narrates the majority of an entire novel about a character who is neither of these bears further scrutiny. Doing so helps us understand why Yunior is so fascinated with Oscar.

While it is true that Yunior learns of Oscar only through his pursuit of Lola, Oscar's sister, soon enough Yunior is consumed by his friendship with Oscar and his biographical details. Yunior and Lola's relationship reads like many of the other stories Yunior tells, particularly in *This Is How You Lose Her*. In fact, those sections in the novel that detail the couple's ultimately failed relationship align with Díaz's more recent collection of stories. Lola narrates a major part of *Oscar Wao*, the section titled "Wildwood." Her narrative serves to highlight the tenacity of her mother, Belicia Cabral, a major character in the novel. So, despite Yunior's occasional diversions into his relationship woes with Lola, the novel's center, its hub, is Oscar. But because Yunior narrates the story, he becomes an important character in the novel by default; everything we learn of Oscar and his family comes through Yunior's own experience and attempts to understand some aspects of Oscar's life, of which he has no direct knowledge. Yunior's narration, therefore, at times lies in the shadow of conjecture and is of great critical value. Further, Jennifer Harford Vargas identifies the multivalent relationship between dictators and authors in *Oscar Wao* that is indicative of both creation and control:

Establishing a similitude between writers and dictators, *The Brief*
Wondrous Life of Oscar Wao grapples with how to circumnavigate
*autho*ritarianism . . . the precarious link among authorship, authority,
and authoritarianism. The novel plays on the tensions between the
two definitions of *dictate*: on the one hand, to order or command
authoritatively and absolutely and, on the other hand, to speak aloud
words that are to be written down or transcribed. There are two types
of competing dictators at the center of [*Oscar Wao*]: the political
dictator (Rafael Trujillo) who rules over the subjects of his regime
and the narrative dictator (Yunior) who retrospectively recounts the
novel's events. As the primary narrator and storyteller, Yunior loosely
functions as a dictator in both senses because he controls and orders
representation and because he collects, writes down and reshapes a
plethora of oral stories that have been recounted to him."[9]

The dyad of Yunior and Oscar drives much of what is possible in
the novel regarding dictators and the fantastic. Elena Machado-Sáez
identifies how "the relationship between Yunior and Oscar calls
attention to how narrating a diaspora's history also entails domes-
ticating difference. While Oscar is endearingly inauthentic, Yunior's
mission to identify him as a representative subject who can embody
the Dominican diaspora leads him ultimately to silence Oscar's points
of queer Otherness—his virginity and sentimentality."[10] Seemingly
an odd couple, there is a more-than-discernable note of poignancy
that runs throughout the novel as the portrait of this friendship
develops. Yunior strikes a tragicomic tone in narrating the tale of a
lovable loser, a guy whose physical attributes and cultural moorings
make him repulsive to the women he encounters. In turn, Oscar helps
readers understand Yunior by being such an antithesis to Dominican
masculinity. Still, despite their clear differences, Yunior and Oscar
are quite alike, perhaps more similar than Yunior would ever care to
admit. For example, they are both drawn to the fantastic, the strange,
the speculative. Oscar is near-obsessed with apocalyptic literature; it

turns out he has drafted several manuscripts in the genre. Similarly, Yunior, as revealed in the story "Miss Lora" from *This Is How You Lose Her*, is also consumed with stories of the coming nuclear apocalypse of the 1980s that never happened. So fascinated is Yunior by end-of-the-world fiction, television, and film that he consistently has dreams about the apocalypse. Thus, in many ways that may not be readily apparent, Yunior is the perfect person to write about Oscar's life.

NARRATION IN *OSCAR WAO*

The more Díaz employs Yunior as a narrator, the more robust the character becomes. In telling other people's stories, he cannot help but narrate about himself. Over time, these tiny personal details and foibles accrete to make him both intriguing and complex. There is a sort of malleability imbued in Yunior that Díaz must undoubtedly find appealing about him as a narrator. This chimeric quality to Yunior, which Katherine Weese views in the light of the narratological concept of unnatural narration, is one of the key reasons that he is such a compelling and engaging narrator. Weese claims that Yunior "increasingly emphasizes the limits of his narratorial powers, which he has earlier flaunted through his first-person omniscient stance and by partially masking his own position as a homodiegetic narrator and assuming the guise of a heterodiegetic, authorial narrator. He thereby implicitly critiques the 'gender work' of the totalitarian regime and allows for the emergence of other masculinities against the hegemonic hyper-masculinity so predominantly displayed by the male characters in [*Oscar Wao*], revealing it to be 'unnatural.'"[11]

In addition to Yunior's dynamic narratorial shifts of position, he has other important facets that make him a noteworthy contribution to studies of literature in the United States. One of these personal traits hinted at in *Drown* now surfaces as a matter of importance: the African heritage to which many Dominican Americans belong. Thus, Díaz's creation of an Afro-Latino author/narrator that foregrounds issues of Afrolatinidad in his stories is a notable development in

Latino/a literature. Because Díaz's novel is wide-ranging in its subject matter, seamlessly interweaving world history, languages, comic book lore, literary knowledge, and science fiction and fantasy in order to construct its narrative worlds, Yunior must be the one who is equipped to speak on these matters due to the restrictions of first-person narration. What strikes me as worth noting is how Yunior, as an author in his own right, sets about the business of narrative worldmaking. Indeed, Díaz's characters and narrators all strive to actuate their differing (and at times competing) agendas as Afro-Latinos in both the United States and the Dominican Republic. In doing so, Díaz creates fictional Afro-Latinos (as opposed to, say, Piri Thomas's representation of himself in his autobiography, *Down These Mean Streets*) who are written into existence by another Afro-Latino (i.e., Yunior). Attending to Díaz's creation of an author/narrator, with his particularized renditions of Afrolatinidad, illuminates how Díaz seeks to inscribe the African *página en blanco*[12] of Dominican culture with a significant representation of Afro-Latinos in US fiction. Ultimately, his manufacture of Afro-Latino characters with the power to write their own story, as well as the story of *other* Afro-Latinos, affirms the power of an author, and fiction more generally, to bring to light what the historical record omits.

To be sure, Díaz's depictions of blackness within his fiction indicate a crucial authorial decision that acknowledges a long-ignored fact that affects the vast majority of Dominicans and Dominican Americans; namely, that a large number of them are undeniably descendants of Africans. Díaz, however, goes one step further and has an Afro-Latino author/narrator choose the lives of other Afro-Latinos as his narrative subject. What makes this narrative decision so powerful is that Dominicans tend not to dwell on their African legacy, generally speaking. Regarding this quandary, Antonio Olliz Boyd observes, "The world of the Afro Latin is always unstable when it comes to questions of color and race. Hence, for the creative artist, emphasis on pigmentation and physical features becomes a ready-made device to express subjective imagery of race or ethnicity, especially for the individual that understands the aesthetics of the Afro Latin space."[13] Thus the fictional narratives of Afro-Latinos in the United States (relatively few as they are) provide a crucial locus not only for conceiving of how conceptions and representations of blackness permeate writing practices situated within both their Dominican and American cultures but also for exploring how these fictional representations have helped change the conversation on Afrolatinidad itself. Díaz places an Afro-Dominican family at the center of his novel, simultaneously foregrounding their African heritage while vilifying the Negrophobia they experience, which reflects the political and ideological power structures in the Dominican Republic, the nexus of which is the Trujillato. As Juanita Heredia notes, "Díaz focuses on the stories of the people in the community, especially the memory of Oscar's family across transnational borders" as opposed to relying on "official sources" to provide an alternative to the historical record.[14]

For Dominican history is fraught with incongruities, and Díaz empowers Yunior to take the challenge directly. Historically, there was a strong push against the predominance of blackness that purportedly threatened the Dominican Republic in the late nineteenth century—specifically in the form of Haitian immigration. This influx of black Haitians "signified the negation of any national dreams of whitening—dreams that, given the overwhelmingly mulatto character of the national population, and the country's inability to attract European immigration, were already doomed to failure but that, doubtless for those very reasons, were deeply cherished."[15] The consequences of the efforts of whitening, or *blanqueamiento*, were, in effect, a genocide of Haitian and Haitian-descended people living in the Dominican Republic in 1937—a seminal event that has made its way into several recent novels despite the nearly seven decades that have passed in the interim.[16] Considering this troubled Dominican history, the noted scholar of Dominican studies Silvio Torres-Saillant notes:

The African-descended majority of the Dominican population will
benefit greatly from a model that allows them to perceive their ances-
tors as *the real protagonist of the epic of the Dominican experience.* Seeing
their progenitors shaping the course that the country's history took,
getting in touch with themselves as a social force that never played
the minutely marginal role ascribed to it by plantocratic historiography, will induce in African-descended Dominicans a vital degree
of historical self-recognition. With that weapon, even if they hold
on to their open concept of race, they will at least feel the wish to
put a stop to notions of Dominicanness that detract from their own
massive presence in the society.[17]

The creation of a protagonist of the epic of the Dominican experience is what Díaz does in *Oscar Wao.* By placing an Afro-Dominican
family at the heart of the story told by Yunior, who is himself
Afro-Dominican, empowering the fictional author with the force of
narrative and history itself, Díaz figuratively takes the spyglass from
Dominicans who look longingly to Spain as a progenitor of their
ancestry and culture and points it squarely at Africa, accomplishing
this deft move by prominently situating Afro-Latinos onto Yunior's
narrative canvas.

In *Oscar Wao,* Yunior narrates the tragic events that surround the
family of Oscar de León, the Oscar "Wao" of the novel's title. Oscar
is the ultimate outcast figure, an outsider even among his Dominican
compatriots. Yunior, despite his penchant for womanizing, is in love
with Oscar's sister Lola and recounts the various circumstances that
lead to Oscar's demise. Yunior is unable to do so coherently, however, without piecing together the personal history of Oscar's mother,
Belicia, or Beli, which in turn necessitates an exploration of Beli's
parents, Abelard and Socorro Cabral, a prominent couple in Dominican society during the dictatorship of Rafael Trujillo. The entire novel
suggests that nation, immigration, and family history are forever
enmeshed. Beli appropriately links the Dominican Republic at the

height of Trujillo's power to her son Oscar, the lowly American-born Dominican outcast who aspires to be a mythmaker like J. R. R. Tolkien, or a master of genre fiction like Stephen King. Oscar's story is simultaneously absurd and heartfelt.

One of Yunior's character traits is his yearning to construct narrative worlds, as we have already seen in many of the stories in *Drown*. Often Yunior is portrayed in a harsh light, especially in stories that take place when he is an adult. However, the one activity that seems to make Yunior a more palatable person is his desire to tell stories, and specifically, to become what Oscar calls a "real writer" (30). While *Drown* features stories that recount either Yunior's childhood or the experiences of his young adulthood, in *Oscar Wao* readers discover that Yunior's project is to bring Oscar's life and genealogy into a larger, perhaps less transient, existence through the careful scaffolding of the book he has written—the book we hold in our hands when we read *Oscar Wao*. Of course, Yunior is a character narrator, but unambiguously, he is a narrator actively engaged in the writing process. In other words, Yunior claims to be the author of *The Brief Wondrous Life of Oscar Wao*. For Yunior, his book is not a novel—a work of fiction. Rather, it is more of a testimonial or tribute, a hagiography for someone deserving of admiration and respect.

This fact adds Yunior to a relatively small group of similar characters in American fiction—a group that most famously includes F. Scott Fitzgerald's Nick Carraway, Ken Kesey's Chief Bromden, and Philip Roth's Nathan Zuckerman, as Ben Railton has noted.[18] Each of these character narrators desires to tell someone else's story, and each of them has a different reason for doing so. Carraway believes that he alone understands Gatsby, and he certainly cannot understand how Gatsby's greatness went ignored by so many people. There is a certain mystery that leads Carraway to take up the events surrounding Gatsby's final days into some coherent narrative. Randall Patrick McMurphy is a mystery to Bromden as well, but for Bromden, McMurphy stands as a testament to the power of resisting institutional authority. Thus, Bromden's narrative is both a memorial and a narrative monument for the sacrificial McMurphy. However, while both Nick and Bromden have in common with Yunior the need to memorialize through narration, it is with Nathan Zuckerman that Yunior has the strongest affinity. Both Zuckerman and Yunior are writers devoted to the craft of narrative worldmaking (Zuckerman, like his creator Philip Roth, is a successful novelist; Yunior is a creative writing teacher at a prestigious university, like *his* creator). In both *American Pastoral* and *The Human Stain*, Zuckerman cannot resist weaving a narrative around an individual charismatic figure (Seymour "Swede" Levov and Coleman Silk, respectively) in an effort to understand how these great men fell from such lofty heights. Zuckerman uses narrative, along with his imagination, to plausibly fill in the gaps created by the historical record surrounding both Levov and Silk.

Yunior, likewise, writes his book in order to make sense of Oscar de León's life leading up to his final years, though he is ambiguous as to why he feels compelled to write his book. Initially, Yunior proposes that his book might serve as a "counterspell," or zafa, to the fukú curse. To me, this seems an unsatisfactory impetus for writing the book, for several reasons. First, why would Yunior be under the shadow of the Cabral/de León family fukú? Why would he need his own counterspell for Oscar's curse when clearly any bit of misfortune can be attributed to fukú? Second, Yunior confesses that by writing the book he acquiesces to the disturbing dream of Oscar that he frequently has. There seems to be a great deal of conscience clearing involved in Yunior's project, to say the least.

At any rate, in order to truly narrate Oscar's demise, Yunior must retroactively recount the events of Oscar's family history, especially within the fukú paradigm. Furthermore, the fukú curse is as intimately connected to Africa as it is to Oscar's family. Díaz, while refraining from taking a didactic perspective regarding the injustices of race, nevertheless boldly acknowledges the African legacy of his Dominican culture through wry, self-deprecating humor, hip-hop language, and the creation of characters who are extremely dark-skinned in ways that prevent them from easy assimilation within the larger hegemonic group. Oscar is an exemplar of the difficulties of assimilation. In short, although Díaz could have followed in the tradition of his birth nation and "whitened" his protagonists and narrators, he in fact does the opposite, revealing the African roots of his characters. Although Díaz does privilege the Latinidad (or Hispanicity) of his culture just as Dominican culture generally does, he nonetheless gives a greater acknowledgement to the African origins of Dominicans, not just by including Afro-Latino characters in his fiction but by endowing Afro-Latinos with the power to create narrative worlds. He achieves all of this while suggesting how his characters orient to a panethnic identity within an America that by and large wishes on the one hand to reduce its citizens to skin color while on the other hand to encourage a silent assimilation into the hegemonic group.

Recall that throughout a majority of the stories in *Drown* there is a deliberate depiction and emphasis of the African phenotype. In "Ysrael," Yunior narrates how his older brother, Rafa, teased him incessantly with various insults as a child, saying, "Most of them had to do with my complexion, my hair, the size of my lips. It's the Haitian, he'd say to his buddies. Hey Señor Haitian, Mami found you on the border and only took you in because she felt sorry for you."[19] In "Fiesta, 1980," Yunior describes his uncle Miguel, who "was about seven feet tall and had his hair combed up and out, into a demi-fro."[20] "How to Date a Browngirl, Blackgirl, Whitegirl, or Halfie" has arguably the most sustained engagement with race as the narrator insists, "Take down any embarrassing photos of your family in the campo, especially the one with the half-naked kids dragging a goat on a rope leash. The kids are your cousins and by now they're old enough to understand why you're doing what you're doing. Hide the pictures of yourself with an Afro."[21]

Just as the narrator in "How to Date" exhorts himself to remove as much evidence of his heritage as possible, there are some things that cannot be hidden easily, such as one's hair. Even more troubling is the narrator's admission that the African blood that flows through the body of a Dominican is nothing more than a regrettable fact that ultimately must be ignored or disregarded. We ought not to miss the point that Yunior's purpose is not the same as Díaz's. While Yunior often derides the African ancestry within his people, Díaz's creation of a character that acknowledges this fact (even if it is to hold it in derision) is a major achievement. Indeed, as Birkhofer asserts, "Caribbean diasporic authors use literature as a medium through which to explore a painful past. More often than not, the 'official history' of the island does not allow the survivors of violence to voice their loss or to mourn the ones who did not survive."[22] The history of blackness is one such painful past that has been neither celebrated nor mourned, and, utilizing a distinct method of hyperbolically representing blackness in his fiction, Díaz showcases the type of nuanced position a Dominican immigrant to the United States must take. When this painful past, expunged as it has been throughout the historical record, is suddenly reinscribed, we take notice. In *Oscar Wao* Díaz employs an Afro-Latino character in the recovery of a great many things thought lost in the novel.

PÁGINAS BLANCAS

Díaz often uses the motif of blankness or erasure as a recurring feature in his fiction. In *Drown*, the character Ysrael is forced to wear a nondescript mask to hide his disfigurement, and his covering serves as a source of both curiosity and poignancy in two separate stories. In *Oscar Wao* Oscar's mother, Beli, often gazes at a man without a face during the most traumatic events of her life. Later she dreams that her foster father, who scarred her back with a skillet of hot oil when she was a child, had a face that "turned blank at the moment he picked up the skillet" (261). Indeed, there is an evident link between a personified blankness and trauma throughout *Oscar Wao*. Yunior also briefly recounts the events surrounding a Columbia graduate student named Jesús de Galíndez, who writes a doctoral dissertation on the dictatorial era of Rafael Leónidas Trujillo Molina. Subsequently, Galíndez disappears, presumably murdered by the Dominican dictator himself. Perhaps not surprisingly, Galíndez's dissertation vanishes as well. In point of fact, Galíndez is an actual, historical figure who did disappear after writing a dissertation that exposed Trujillo for what he was. Díaz's invocation of this historical intertext demonstrates how he incorporates elements from history and from fantasy, revealing how both are comfortable within the same spaces. "What more sci-fi than Santo Domingo? What more fantasy than the Antilles?" Oscar asks Yunior (6).

There are other moments of erasure in the novel. According to Yunior, Abelard Cabral, Oscar's maternal grandfather, is tortured, killed, and effectively erased because of a book he was writing on Trujillo. The only extant copy of Abelard's exposé disappears. Finally, near the end of the novel, Oscar writes a manuscript that purports to explain "everything" to Yunior only for it to go missing after Oscar is murdered, never having reached Yunior. Yunior later has dreams for years after Oscar's death in which Oscar wears "a wrathful mask that hides his face but behind the eyeholes I see a familiar pair of close-set eyes" and has hands that "are seamless" as he invites Yunior to examine a book he is holding for him to see, until Yunior realizes "the book's pages are blank" (325). Díaz's continual allusions to these and other instances of erasure, what he calls the *páginas en blanco*, remind the reader that there is always some aspect of Díaz's fiction (and consequently, Dominican history) that keeps full knowledge just out of a reader's reach. As a result, Yunior consistently struggles to supply narrative material to fill these lacunae.

In truth, Yunior is fascinated by both writers and writing. His passion for writing is unsurprising, as he has taken on the task of creating a narrative, and his self-reflexive musings on the process of writing provide him with an additional dimension for critical analysis.

In other words, Yunior is not just a narrator who recounts events he has witnessed or stories he has heard. It is clear that he constructs a narrative by putting words onto the page, a fact of which he is acutely aware. This fact becomes especially relevant as he provides repeated examples of the silencing of writers. Despite the frustrating inability of these articulate personages and characters to write a final, finished product, there is one writer who does manage to write with impunity, and write prolifically—a writer whom Yunior discusses at length in footnote nine—Dominican Republic President Joaquín Balaguer:

> Although not essential to our tale, per se, Balaguer is essential to the Dominican one, so therefore we must mention him, even though I'd rather piss in his face. . . . In the days of the Trujillato, Balaguer was just one of El Jefe's more efficient ringwraiths. Much is made of his intelligence (he certainly impressed the Failed Cattle Thief) and of his asceticism (when *he* raped his little girls he kept it real quiet). . . . It was he who oversaw/initiated the thing we call Diaspora. Considered our national "genius," Joaquín Balaguer was a Negrophobe, an apologist to genocide, an election thief, and a killer of people who wrote better than himself, famously ordering the death of journalist Orlando Martínez. Later, when he wrote his memoirs, he claimed he knew who had done the foul deed (not him, of course) and left a blank page, a página en blanco, in the text to be filled in with the truth upon his death. (Can you say *impunity*?) Balaguer died in 2002. The página is still blanca. (90)

Several key points in Yunior's footnote can help focus our understanding of the dynamic between power, writing, and race in *Oscar Wao*. The historical record reveals Balaguer to be a productive writer who wrote in many genres, including poetry, narrative fiction, biography, and autobiography. In short, unlike Trujillo, Balaguer was a real intellectual. Because of his close affiliation to Trujillo and his rise to Dominican power, Balaguer represents the powers of writing at their worst. According to Yunior, Balaguer, insecure in his writing, ordered the murder of other writers. Further, Balaguer provided the impetus for Dominican diaspora, which, of course, has a direct bearing on Oscar's family, specifically his mother, Beli. And, hypocritically in Yunior's eyes, Balaguer self-censures his memoir by silencing himself in order to appear as a more sympathetic figure. The result is that the two brutal dictators described in *Oscar Wao* delight in silencing writers while promoting Negrophobic agendas with ease. One of Yunior's charges, it seems, is to substantiate the African legacy of Dominicans as well as to create the narrative of Oscar's family by proxy.

According to Yunior, it is Abelard who initiates the fukú curse that will plague his progeny. Yunior attributes Trujillo's violence against Abelard to one of two things: 1) Abelard did not readily offer up his beautiful daughters when Trujillo desired it or 2) Abelard had written a book that claimed Trujillo's supernaturalism. That Trujillo would go to such lengths in order to punish a rebuke was a commonly held belief among the Dominican community. On this subject, Yunior states: "There's one of these bellaco tales in almost everybody's hometown. It's one of those easy stories because in essence *it explains it all.* Trujillo took your houses, your properties, put your pops and your moms in jail? Well, it was because he wanted to fuck the beautiful daughter of the house! And your family wouldn't let him!" (244). However, Yunior is not interested in "easy stories." Like his "compañero" Oscar, he is attracted to the "speculative genres" (43). For Yunior, the sheer might and vigor of the Cabral/de León fukú suggest that it is the result of more than merely another "bellaco" tale. Rather, Abelard's "grimoire," or book of magic, (as Yunior describes it) was set to expose Trujillo's other-worldliness. Thus, just as Balaguer ordered the death of journalist Orlando Martínez, Trujillo imposes a fukú upon Abelard and his family because of a book:

> Sometime in 1944 (so the story goes), while Abelard was still worried about whether he was in trouble with Trujillo, he started writing a book about—what else?—Trujillo. By 1945 there was

already a tradition of ex-officials writing tell-all books about the Trujillo regime. But that apparently was not the kind of book Abelard was writing. His shit, if we are to believe the whispers, was an exposé of the supernatural roots of the Trujillo regime! A book about the Dark Powers of the President, a book in which Abelard argued that the tales the common people told about the president—that he was supernatural, that he was not human—may in some ways have been true. That it was possible that Trujillo was, if not in fact, then in principle, a creature from another world! (245)

"The Lost Final Book of Dr. Abelard Luis Cabral" (246), along with his entire library and every bit of his handwriting, vanishes, leaving Yunior and Oscar wishing they could have read Cabral's grimoire. Instead, Yunior sets about to create his own book that bridges Abelard's project with Oscar's longing to be the "Dominican Tolkien." Despite the many writers who have been silenced, Yunior strives to have his story fill the void created by dictators and curses alike. As a result, Yunior's decision to write a book is one that bears great risk. Call it fukú.

BLACK EVE

As Torres-Saillant observes regarding the mulatto presence in the Dominican Republic, Dominicans are all the descendants of a white Adam (the privileged European of early Hispaniola) and black Eve (the desired African woman). He attributes a great power to this black Eve figure, for it is *her* African phenotype that dominates present-day Afro-Dominicans. It is no wonder that the character of Díaz's novel with the deepest fortitude is not Oscar or Yunior (despite both of their privileged positions as writers and men), but instead, Oscar's mother Beli, a voluptuous, goddess-like, self-assured, Afro-Dominican woman. She is the unacknowledged presence of Africa that Torres-Saillant discusses in his essay. She functions as a stand-in for the black Eve of Dominican history within *Oscar Wao*. In Beli,

Díaz creates the real protagonist of what is ostensibly the epic of Dominican experience in America, and he charges Yunior with narrating her significant story. As a result, Beli functions as a conduit from Third World to First World because she represents the Dominican diaspora, but that is not all. In a novel of 335 pages, Yunior devotes a section of nearly ninety pages to Beli and her coming-of-age story. Hers is a story that not only provides context for the lives of her two children, Lola and Oscar, but also constitutes an important strand of the larger narrative. Later, in a section that recounts the series of events that leads to the death of nearly all of Beli's family, she takes a key role in the narrative once more—in sections that occupy the center of the text. While Yunior repeatedly concentrates on writers and writing, he reserves a prominent place in his narrative for Beli— a woman who is not a writer, but one who is a creator nonetheless. In the midst of silencing, disappearing, and murder, Beli's story is atypical in her family in that she survives to produce something tangible in the world. She is a crucial figure in both Oscar's life and Yunior's narrative. Accordingly, her centrality allows her to serve as a stand-in for a symbolic black Eve for Afro-Dominicans.

Beli's African ancestry is no secret. And this fact, for her family at least, foreshadows the trials and tribulations that await them all: "The family claims the first sign was that Abelard's third and final daughter, given the light early on in her father's capsulization, was born black. And not just any kind of black. But *black* black—kongoblack, shangoblack, kaliblack, zapoteblack, rekhablack—and no amount of fancy Dominican racial legerdemain was going to obscure the fact. That's the kind of culture I belong to: people took their child's black complexion as an ill omen" (248). This issue with blackness is part of a larger history within Dominican history. In his discussion of a symbolic black Eve in Dominican history, Torres-Saillant cites the narrative of Gaspar Arredondo y Pichardo, "a slave-owning landholder from eastern Hispaniola who lost his economic and social rank with Toussaint's unification of the island in 1801 and then recounted what he saw as the ignominy of former slaves who were suddenly of equal social status."[23] Torres-Saillant notes that, in order to illustrate his fall from social grace (rather than applaud the raising of an oppressed people to his own level), Arredondo y Pichardo, a white creole, often narrated the occasion when he was obligated to dance with a former slave at a ball. Using this image of a white man dancing with a black woman as an interracial first couple—a type of Adam and Eve for the Dominican Republic—Torres-Saillant argues that, based on the phenotype of their descendants, it is to black Eve that the majority of Dominicans owe a substantial aspect of their ancestry. Thus, "of their two moral legacies, that is, his mournful pain at the inability to continue enslaving other people versus her proud dignity as she faces her former master on the same social level, hers constitutes a far more humanizing and empowering heritage to the Dominican people."[24] However, despite her strong presence in her progeny's physiognomy, black Eve (i.e., the heritage of blackness) is often largely ignored in Dominican culture. It is akin to ignoring an important matriarch in your family.

Yunior's project seeks to rectify this disparity. Beli's skin is extremely dark, and Yunior emphasizes this time and again, describing her as "so dark it was as if the Creatrix had, in her making, blinked" (77). Even Baní, the city in which Beli lives during her youth, Yunior narrates, is "famed for its resistance to blackness, and it was here, alas, that the darkest character in our story resided" (78). In Díaz's fiction, it is apparent that the darker the skin of a character, the more tribulation the character will experience either through societal mores or a sort of learned helplessness that amounts to self-loathing. As a youth, after the assassination of her immediate family resulting from Abelard's defiance of Trujillo, Beli falls into the hands of negligent relatives. Her father's cousin, La Inca, eventually saves Beli from her horrid circumstance. During her years in school, Beli is an outcast, along with "the Boy in the Iron Lung, the idiot, and the Chinese girl named Wei" but even Wei ridicules Beli's skin: "You black, she said, fingering Belicia's thin forearm. *Black*-black" (84). Beli does not allow her dark skin or outsider status (something she inadvertently passes on to her son Oscar) to keep her from attaining what she wants. Puberty enables Beli to become the center of attention wherever she goes, and when she suddenly realizes the implicit (and explicit) power of her voluptuousness, the world changes for her:

> Beli, who'd been waiting for something exactly like her body her whole life, was sent *over the moon* by what she now knew. By the undeniable concreteness of her desirability which was, in its own way, Power. Like the accidental discovery of the One Ring. Like stumbling into the wizard Shazam's cave or finding the crashed ship of the Green Lantern! Hypatía Belicia Cabral finally had power and a true sense of self. . . . Telling Beli not to flaunt those curves would have been like asking the persecuted fat kid not to use his recently discovered mutant abilities. With great power comes great responsibility . . . *bullshit*. Our girl ran into the future that her new body represented and never ever looked back. (94)

Empowered by her voluptuous body, Beli sets her sights on Jack Pujols, "the school's handsomest (read: whitest) boy, a haughty slender melnibonian of pure European stock whose cheeks looked like they'd been knapped by a master and whose skin was unflawed by scar, mole, blemish, or hair, his small nipples were the pink perfect ovals of sliced salchicha" (89). Pujols is a stand-in for the entitlement and privilege of the Trujillo regime and whiteness, and Beli is utterly infatuated with Pujols, pursuing him "with the great deliberation of Ahab after you-know-who. (And of all these things the albino boy was the symbol. Wonder ye then at the fiery hunt?)" (95). Beli does manage to live her life without him, deciding to look beyond the promise of being loved by and married to a white man, undoubtedly a desire for *blanqueamiento*.

Beli's second heartbreak (she has three, we are told), comes at the hands of a man known only as the Gangster, a "middle-aged Caliban who dyed his hair and had a thatch of curlies on his back and shoulders. More like a third-base umpire than an Avatar of her Glorious Future" (124), the antithesis of Jack Pujols. The Gangster is a black Dominican, who has inveigled his way to power and influence as a way of erasing his blackness. Despite his dark skin, utterly unappealing for even the dark-skinned Beli, he manages to romance his way into her heart. Of the Gangster, Yunior narrates, "He escorted her to the most exclusive restaurants of the capital, took her to the clubs that had never tolerated a nonmusician prieto inside their door before (dude was that powerful—to break the injunction against *black*). . . . In other words, he exposed her to the fucking world (at least the one circumscribed by the DR)" (124). In fact, the Gangster proves to be not only married, but married to Trujillo's sister, a seeming impossibility that Yunior casually explains thus: "Did you really think some street punk from Samaná was going to reach the upper echelons of the Trujillato on hard work alone? Negro, please—this ain't a fucking comic book!" (138).

Pregnant and now discovered by the Gangster's wife, Belicia brings the powers of Trujillo down upon her head. "They beat her like she was a slave. Like she was a dog" (147), Yunior recounts. It is her hate that keeps her alive, the realization that the Gangster had tricked her. Comparing her to perhaps the most famous (and influential) superhero of all time, Yunior concludes, "Like Superman in *The Dark Knight Returns*, who drained from an entire jungle the photonic energy he needed to survive Coldbringer, so did our Beli resolve out of her anger her own survival. In other words, her coraje saved her life" (149). Beli's exodus from the Dominican Republic coincides with the fall of the Trujillato, and though she has endured so much, "she is sixteen and her skin is the darkness before the black, the plum of the day's last light, her breasts like sunsets trapped beneath her skin, but for all her youth and beauty she has a sour distrusting expression that only dissolves under the weight of immense pleasure" (164). Given the Trujillato's all-too-successful efforts at erasing blackness and resistance, Beli's perseverance is admirable if not astonishing.

While the majority of Díaz's stories published before the release of *Oscar Wao* tend to reference blackness and Africanness in a self-deprecatory manner, as in the story "How to Date," the moral strength of the characters in *Oscar Wao* is directly correlated to the darkness of their skin. Hence, as Beli is the "darkest character" of the novel, she is also the most fiercely independent and strong-willed character as well. Beli is a force of will and determination, despite her father, mother, and two older sisters being murdered—considered collateral damage of the Trujillo dictatorship—along with her literally being sold as a baby to a family of negligent incompetents and later burned with hot oil as a young girl. Her story shows her overcoming incredible antagonism that manifests in any number of forms. Beli ultimately is a product of Dominican prejudice and racism against its dark-skinned citizens. However, her desirability conflates her character with black Eve and thus she symbolically serves as the matriarch of a line of Dominican Americans. Though Díaz, through his narrator, Yunior, continually draws attention to Beli's dark skin—noting that she is called "La Prieta Quemada"—*prieta* meaning a woman with dark skin, and *quemada* meaning someone who is burned (261)—as well as the skin of her children, Díaz does not permit this potential shortcoming to limit her possibilities within either Dominican or American society. In fact, Yunior seems unabashedly impressed by Beli's strength and determination.

Conversely, Díaz creates a nearly insuperable obstacle for Beli and her family to overcome, one that is the engine for Yunior's narrative. Throughout *Oscar Wao* Beli's complications in life stem from the fukú curse mentioned at the outset of the novel, a near-supernatural force that inhibits Dominicans—and specifically dark-skinned Afro-Dominicans—from achieving a stronger sense of black identity. Since the fukú curse arrives from Africa as a result of Columbus's voyage to Hispaniola, it seems that the African curse functions as a retaliation for the subjugation of its people. It thus follows that the darkest characters in Díaz's novel are tested in a nearly Job-like manner. Or perhaps it is that, like Job, Beli—as well as Oscar, for that matter—is continually able to get up after being knocked down again and again. In fact, the biblical figure that better serves as Beli's analog is Jacob, a comparison Díaz, through Yunior, initiates by saying of Beli, "at night she struggled Jacob-like against the ocean pressing down on her" (89).

Genesis 32:24–36:43 recounts Jacob's struggle with an unknown figure during the darkness of night. The battle ends in a stalemate as the stranger asks to be released as dawn breaks. Jacob will not release the stranger unless the man gives him a blessing. The man, revealed to be an angel, renames Jacob as Israel, and later God tells him, "Be fruitful and multiply; A nation and a company of nations shall come from you." That Beli, the "Queen of Diaspora" (261), leaves for America makes the connection to Jacob even stronger, for Jacob, too, fled his homeland for fear of being murdered. Further, Beli's exile to America is possible only through La Inca's strength of spirit and resolve that convince Beli to leave. The difficulty in convincing Beli to leave allows Yunior to parallel La Inca with the story of Jacob as well, this time as the one whom Jacob wrestles: "La Inca wrestled with herself those long nights! But which side was Jacob and which side was the Angel?" (158). Perhaps La Inca serves as an Angel to Beli's Jacob. As both an Eve and Jacob figure, Beli has the potential of serving as the headwaters for a flood of Afro-Dominican Americans. And when Yunior aligns Beli to Anacaona under the trope of the dark beauty obsessed by men in power, he completes an analogous triumvirate that combines tribulation, beauty, and strength. As Díaz relates in footnote twenty-nine, Anacaona is known as "the Golden Flower. One of the Founding Mothers of the New World and the most beautiful Indian in the World" despite her Malinche-like status of attempting to bridge her world with the European (244). That Yunior exalts Beli to this status after the fact (for he is, after all, reconstructing this narrative) is a testament to his respect for her as a matriarchal figure for Dominican diaspora.

In *Drown* and *The Brief Wondrous Life of Oscar Wao*, then, Díaz uses humor and a streetwise pragmatism to approach the long-ignored issue of blackness in Dominican culture. What may have limited someone like Beli before—the fact that she's a prieta—now no longer has as much of an influence as it may once have had in Dominican culture. Thus, by creating an Afro-Dominican champion to tell the stories of such dark-skinned Dominicans as Beli, Lola, and Oscar, Díaz takes a notable and crucial step in acknowledging Africa within Dominican culture and, perhaps, has initiated the first bold pen strokes in writing the *página en blanco* of an entire people who no longer have to shamefully hide the pictures that reflect this often unrecognized aspect of their history.

Despite this approach of giving voice to the struggles of a particular type of person who has by and large been ignored by Dominican society, Díaz does not allow Yunior to fall into sentimentality or saccharine happily-ever-afters. In the end, Beli succumbs to breast cancer, so that, tragically, that which empowered her to begin with becomes her downfall. Her son Oscar is murdered because he obstinately loved the wrong woman and could not understand that he did not need to prove he was Dominican. Yet Oscar feels he must, as he is continually plagued with questions of self, patrimony, and nationalism. Who is a Dominican? What does it mean to be Dominican, much less a Dominican American? How are they to self-identify? Oscar does not seem to know the answers to these questions, and neither does Yunior. *The Brief Wondrous Life of Oscar Wao* is a novel that displays this inability to define oneself in America at the start of the twenty-first century. But is the outlook for Dominican Americans so bleak? The novel's ending provides a clue.

BRIEF, NAMELESS LIVES

Lola is the lone survivor of the Cabral/de León family. She, like her mother, continues the lineage of the once-prestigious family. Like Oscar and Yunior, she takes up writing as a means of coping with her situation.²⁵ She states: "On my days off I would drink with Aldo, or I would sit in the sand dressed in all black and try to write in my journal, which I was sure would form the foundation for a utopian society after we blew ourselves into radioactive kibble" (65). Later, Yunior reports that Lola has a child, a daughter he describes as "dark and blindingly fast" (329). Lola's daughter, Isis, is the one who may live to see the fukú curse run its course and finally lose its force; on the other hand, it may continue by claiming her life. Yunior dreams that Isis will "take all we've done and all we've learned and add her own insights and she'll put an end to it" (330–31). As in the first sentence of the novel, "it" seems to refer to fukú. Throughout the novel, fukú has worked its damage on the brief, nameless lives of Oscar's family, and the question is: why? It seems fukú affects those who are at a crossroads of identity, those Dominicans who are descended from Africa but refuse to acknowledge her. Oscar, Belicia, Lola, and even Yunior suffer identity paralysis. However, America provides Dominicans an opportunity to reclaim their African heritage. Already we see this happening in the appropriation of so-called hip-hop language and the use of the word "nigger," both of which appear in abundance in Díaz's fiction. In miniature, this is what Díaz does with the nearly obliterated African heritage of the Dominican Republic. He takes something considered to be verboten within a culture and reappropriates it to suit his fiction. What is more, Díaz is about liberating language. Of his use of the word "nigger," Díaz states in an interview with Rachel Chambers: "As an author you have to ask yourself what do you owe or what is this relationship that you have with this word that has afflicted you your whole life."²⁶ He reflects upon using that word in another interview, this time more directly: "It's one of those things, I mean—there's a ton of child rape in this book too. Does that mean I'm a child rapist, I endorse child rape? I mean, the word *nigger* exists in the world. And some people aren't okay with a Latino writer using it, and you know what? That's really cool! That's the difference that we're talking about, is it real life or is it art? . . .

Or is there something far more complicated going on, with the concept of representations, or the concept of deploying 'taboo' language and who deploys it?"[27] Whether one agrees with his rationale or not, there is little doubt that Díaz trains a spotlight on some of the most vexed issues of race and identity and thereby promotes new ways of engaging with those issues. It is useful in this context to consider Díaz's reflection on the reality of having Barack Obama as president, considering it from the perspective of his best friend's twin children, India and Matteo:

> They will grow up with a black president as their commonplace. I grew up in a world where people in power didn't look anything like me. I grew up in an America that didn't reflect me at all, where I was therefore a ghost. How that affected my psyche and my sense of self there is no telling. India and Matteo, though, will grow up in a world where the most powerful man reflects them back, at least in part. This might mean nothing. It might mean everything. But for the first time in human history we'll have a chance to find out.[28]

Just as Díaz describes himself as a ghost in a land that did not reflect him, the dark-skinned characters of his fiction inhabit a Dominican (and American) culture in which they, too, are ghosts. However, the truth is that Afro-Latinos (Dominican or otherwise) are certainly *not* ghosts in America, and Yunior's project of documenting their lives is a testament to this fact. Afro-Latinos and the stories they both create and inhabit signal the potential for what so many throughout history have feared and worked so hard to keep from coming to fruition: a black planet. Díaz's characters resist dictators, oppression, and curses in the hopes that the next generation will have an opportunity that they did not have. They signal a movement toward the kinds of identities (or at least modes of self-identification) that populate the fiction of Edwidge Danticat, for example. For Yunior, such a move is embodied in the last, best hope for Beli's family, her granddaughter Isis—namesake of the ancient

Egyptian goddess of motherhood and fertility—and the promise of a future she is perhaps destined to fulfill.

Díaz's fiction prominently reminds us that we should continue to broaden our understanding of Latinidad and US Latino/a culture in order to recognize the presence of race in American literature. He accomplishes this by creating Yunior, an Afro-Latino author/narrator who inscribes an erased narrative of Afro-Latinos where historical records do not exist. In this sense, Yunior demonstrates that despite efforts to silence "nerds" who are brave enough to speak out against power, invariably some will succeed in creating a voice with resonance. Díaz's fiction exposes this important area of the Latino/a literary topography, spurring us to rethink further how we conceive of the nexus of Latinidad, race, and nationalism in American literature.

APOCALYPTIC INTERTEXTS

Along with its engagements with race and history, another defining feature of Díaz's novel is its relationship to comic books, science fiction, and fantasy literature. According to Albert Jordy Raboteau, these intertexts "create a penumbra of meaning, a rhetoric of significance and of signifying" in *Oscar Wao*.[29] Though many comics and sci-fi/fantasy novels appear or are obliquely referenced in *Oscar Wao*, few dominate like those of Jack Kirby and J. R. R. Tolkien. Kirby, instrumental in creating some of the most iconic superheroes in comic book lore—the Avengers, the Fantastic Four, the X-Men, the Hulk, and the vibrant Fourth World universe—is clearly an inspirational figure within *Oscar Wao*. Similarly, Tolkien looms large in Yunior's imagination, as well as Oscar's. As Tim Lanzendörfer claims: "Yunior's ambivalence about the fantastic episodes that the novel produces later on must be read against the backdrop of the introduction's establishment of a marvelous past but also in the narrative's insistence on that past's interpretation through the narrator's lens of fantasy, which alone seems capable of explaining that the best approximation of the history of the Dominican Republic is the marvelous reality of fantasy fiction."[30] For his part, Oscar's greatest achievement would be to become a world creator like Tolkien. The stories of Kirby and Tolkien give Oscar and Yunior a means not of escaping the world, but rather a means of *understanding* their world. In short, the fantastical worlds of Kirby and Tolkien provide a context for the "stranger than fiction" quality of Dominican history.

Kirby is a touchstone of the highest order in *Oscar Wao*. Yunior unabashedly calls himself "the Watcher," a character from Kirby's *Fantastic Four* comics, many times throughout the narrative. In footnote ten, Yunior proclaims, "My shout-out to Jack Kirby aside, it's hard as a Third Worlder not to feel a certain amount of affinity for Uatu the Watcher; he resides in the hidden Blue Area of the Moon and we DarkZoners reside (to quote Glissant) on '*la face cache de la Terre*' (Earth's hidden face)" (92). Kirby's storyworlds thus hold great sway over and indeed give shape to Yunior's worldview.

Consider the novel's opening epigraph: "'Of what import are brief, nameless lives . . . to **Galactus**?'" Here, unlike many of the other invocations of intertextual material in *Oscar Wao*, the reader is provided with a very specific citation, "*Fantastic Four*/Stan Lee and Jack Kirby/(Vol. I, No. 49, April 1966)" (n.p.). However, a reader unfamiliar with Galactus will miss the significance of this epigraph entirely. The quote suggests that Díaz is prompting the reader to refer to this particular issue of the *Fantastic Four* precisely because it informs the rest of the novel; that is the function of epigraphs, after all. Just as the excerpt of Derek Walcott's poem "The Schooner *Flight*" shapes a reader's expectation and engagement with *Oscar Wao*, the Fantastic Four's plight with Galactus is equally key.

The quotation originally appears in the middle part of what Charles Hatfield refers to as the "Galactus trilogy," #48–50, which "first introduced the seminal characters Galactus and the Silver Surfer."[31] Hatfield sizes up Galactus as "not so much a villain as an amoral, impersonal force."[32] Indeed, Galactus can devour entire worlds without the capacity to conceive of the "brief, nameless lives" that inhabit the worlds he consumes. That, Hatfield maintains, is the very turning point, or at least point of conflict, in the trilogy— "forcing Galactus, through the Silver Surfer, to *take* notice."[33]

Further, the Watcher himself is an extraterrestrial being with godlike powers (though not to the extent of Galactus), and his role in Kirby's storyworlds is to intercede on behalf of humanity. He, unlike Galactus, can recognize the inherent worth of Earth's inhabitants. Thus by aligning himself with the Watcher, and echoing his title with Galactus's quote regarding the brevity of insignificant lives, Yunior establishes himself as an advocate for the voiceless throughout the narrative—Oscar in particular. He is the Watcher, but he is the narrator as well. Yunior is not only watching, he adopts the godlike power of creating a world through narrative.

In the introduction to his superb critical study on Jack Kirby, *Hand of Fire* (2012), Hatfield invokes an image from Kirby's *The New Gods*: "A wall of white stone stands alone in a barren, wind-whipped field. Rugged yet ageless—unadorned, enigmatic, and still—the wall is a slab higher than any man is tall. A silent sentinel, this slab stands as if waiting. For what? . . . Across the wall, the pyrographic hand inscribes its meaning, transforming blank whiteness into a signifying surface. Its index finger—pointing, writing—is a stylus of fire. The message is so much cosmic calligraphy."[34] Hatfield's creative ekphrasis of Kirby's panel resonates with Yunior's task of inscribing the *página en blanco* in *Oscar Wao*. Hatfield argues that the pilgrim in Kirby's panel "is obviously confronting God, it takes but a little critical nerve to see the wall's provoking whiteness as also the (to a cartoonist) ever-challenging white blankness of the uninscribed page."[35] I would make a very similar point regarding Kirby's influence on Díaz and his narrator. Like Kirby, Yunior cannot abide a blank page.

But perhaps Kirby's most significant influence on Yunior, and of course Díaz, is his "apocalyptic imagination."[36] Again, Hatfield's remarks on this aspect of Kirby's oeuvre are key for understanding Yunior's engagement with apocalypse in *Oscar Wao*: "With its outsized approach to superheroes, the Fourth World gave free reign to Kirby's apocalyptic leanings. Here I have in mind two meanings of *apocalypse*. First is the original sense of the word derived from the Greek *apokalypsis* (revelation), meaning an act of revealing or uncovering. Second is the more modern sense—though a misnomer—meaning a cataclysm, more specifically the end of the world; that is, an eschatological vision of the end of history."[37] In both senses of the word as outlined by Hatfield, *Oscar Wao* is apocalyptic. Yunior attempts to reveal or uncover specific erasures or omissions through the histories that run throughout his narrative, but he also continually emphasizes the idea of cataclysm. Again, Yunior begins his narration by identifying the fukú curse as "uttered just as one world perished and another began" (1). Readers can see the various tragedies that befall the Cabral/de León family as a series of micro-apocalypses that contribute to this larger understanding of the end of history without ever reaching postapocalypse. Oscar confidently maintains that nothing ever ends, citing the panel he circled in his copy of Alan Moore's *Watchmen* in which Dr. Manhattan proclaims, "In the end? Nothing ends, Adrian. Nothing ever ends" (331). This assertion, it would seem, also applies to Yunior's understanding of apocalypse. The more he reveals by attempting to understand the past, the more he understands that apocalypse is a *constant* unfolding of world-ending events. But can the accumulation of apocalypses contribute to some larger purpose we can recognize as good?

In one post–Pulitzer Prize interview, Díaz revealed that he had, in fact, been writing more than just his second book during the interim of years between the publications of his first and his second. "I wrote four books," he explained. In one of these projects, Díaz recalls:

> I was writing a novel about a slightly futuristic American version of what we're living now. In '94, I started writing a novel about an enormous terrorist act that destroyed the United States. The novel takes place twenty years after this destruction, with all the stuff that

we're dealing with now—a dirty war, the disappeared, the concept of terrorism. Anyway, 9/11 happened some years into the process, and I was like, OK, I don't have a novel. The U.S. that I had imagined was nowhere near as crazy and as incredibly damaging and brutal and indifferent as the U.S. that we're currently living in. I thought I was being transgressive, apocalyptic, an out-there person. And then reality lapped me, it just lapped me.[38]

In the wake of 9/11, Díaz's project would not see the light of day. But, like any great fantasist, Díaz was still allured by the concept of a postapocalyptic world. If he wanted to take up postapocalyptic themes in his novel, he would have to retreat from anything remotely connected to the terrorist attacks of 9/11. While many writers in the subsequent post-9/11 years made the attempt to incorporate the surrealism of the event within their storyworlds (with mixed results at best), Díaz infused *Oscar Wao* with an apocalyptic sensibility by grafting his story onto some of the most memorable end-of-the-world narratives available to him. The result was that Díaz penned one of the best-reviewed and highly acclaimed novels in the post-9/11 era.

Díaz's approach in his apocalyptic novel is to create a scaffold of apocalyptic and postapocalyptic intertexts on which he can elevate his story to the level of an epic such as Tolkien's *The Lord of the Rings*. Tolkien himself theorized an aspect of narrating stories that accounts for a sudden turn of events at the story's climax that, borrowing from his Catholic faith, he termed "eucatastrophe."[39] While Tolkien's coinage is sometimes mistaken for the concept of a happy ending, or pejoratively, the deus ex machina, his concept of eucatastrophe in the fairy story may best be understood as a "deep structure of hope," as Susan Johnston has argued.[40] Tolkien further defines eucatastrophe as "a sudden and miraculous grace: never to be counted on to recur."[41]

Eucatastrophe is Tolkien's account for the ending of *The Lord of the Rings*. The quest to destroy the One Ring is taken up by the hobbit Frodo Baggins and his eight companions. After approximately a thousand pages, the reader finds Frodo at the precipice of Orodruin, known as Mount Doom. Like Isildur before him nearly three millennia prior, Frodo cannot bring himself to destroy the One Ring: "'I have come,' he said. 'But I do not choose now to do what I came to do. I will not do this deed. The Ring is mine!'"[42] Frodo's failure here would most certainly have culminated in an apocalypse within Middle Earth were it not for a fortuitous intervention by Gollum—the long-tortured creature who forcibly removes the Ring from Frodo's possession by biting off his finger. In his subsequent moment of ecstasy and elation at having regained possession of the Ring, Gollum "stepped too far, toppled, wavered for a moment on the brink, and then with a shriek he fell. Out of the depths came his last wail *Precious*, and he was gone."[43] The "grace" of having Gollum accomplish the task that Frodo cannot is indeed "sudden and miraculous"; we can expect such an event never to happen again. For some readers, this resolution to such a lengthy saga is somewhat too convenient or lucky.

Here I am interested in the concept of eucatastrophe as a potential alternative to ostensibly catastrophic events within a narrative. Tolkien's explication of his concept of eucatastrophe as it functions in a fairy story, especially as it operates within *The Lord of the Rings*, contributes to an examination of *Oscar Wao* in a way that other apocalyptic intertexts such as *Watchmen* or *The Fantastic Four* within Díaz's novel do not. In short, eucatastrophe suggests an inherent good arising out of what initially appears to be a catastrophic outcome. Above all, it allows us to excavate the deep structure of hope embedded within *Oscar Wao* in spite of the fukú curse that dominates the narrative.

Understanding how Yunior and Oscar view Tolkien's work aids in the excavation of this deep structure of hope in *Oscar Wao*. While Yunior analogizes the ubiquitous threat of pure evil that dominates both Middle Earth and the Dominican Republic in the form of a dictatorial power, Oscar places high value not only on Tolkien's storyworld but also on Tolkien's more fundamental project of creating Middle Earth. Whereas Yunior cannot escape the looming shadow of Sauron or Trujillo and the long reach of evil, Oscar's vision of triumph is one day to be known as "the Dominican Tolkien" (192).

It is significant that both of these Dominican young men admire the sheer craftsmanship of writing and narrative worldmaking, and they engage in this very process. Yunior, for his part, claims not to be interested in the "nerdy" things that drive Oscar, but his writing speaks otherwise. Further, though on the surface Yunior's interests lie with apocalypse—at one point even Oscar compares himself to the Jack Kirby character aptly named Apokalips (170)—we must remember that he claims to want to tell Oscar's story, not his own. Yunior is indignant at the prospect that he might change his story in order to suit expected conventions for this sort of novel: "I know I've thrown a lot of fantasy and sci-fi in the mix but this is supposed to be a *true* account of the Brief Wondrous Life of Oscar Wao" (285). Bearing this fact in mind—that this is Oscar's story—Oscar's take on Tolkien is considerable.

Readers can only fathom Yunior's conception of evil through comparisons with Darkseid and Sauron. For Yunior, the evil with which he is familiar—that of Trujillo—has a parallel only in the most outrageous villains of speculative fiction. In *The Lord of the Rings*, Sauron has been incorporeal ever since Isildur cut the One Ring from the Dark Lord's hand. Sauron having been rendered impotent and with the One Ring thought lost, the fear that preoccupies the wise of Middle Earth is that Sauron will be reunited once more with the One Ring. Such a result would be not only catastrophic but apocalyptic as well.

Indeed, in Tolkien's storyworld, each "Age" coincides with what might be considered an apocalyptic event—one that forever alters the world. For example, Sauron's final defeat, when the One Ring is destroyed in Orodruin, initiates the Fourth Age of Middle Earth. Yunior's appropriation of Tolkien's text is to delineate clearly good from evil. Tolkien invents characters that are uncomplicatedly evil (e.g., Morgoth, Sauron) or good (e.g., Tom Bombadil). Thus, his storyworld works well if one attempts to find analogs of pure good or unadulterated evil. Of course, this type of intertextual knowledge is the inherent challenge for the reader, lest we lose sight of that. A reader without an intimate familiarity of *Lord of the Rings* is destined to miss many of these parallels on which Yunior draws.

But it is Oscar's affinity for Tolkien that makes the most of this particular intertext. It is safe to say that of all the speculative authors admired by Oscar, Tolkien and his world consume Oscar most. Not only does he wish to be the Dominican Tolkien, Oscar consistently works to find similarities between Middle Earth and his own world. When Oscar moves into Yunior's apartment after Oscar's attempted suicide, Yunior says *"Mellon,"* the Sindarin word for "friend," though Yunior claims that this was only the way Oscar remembered that moment (200).[44] And when Oscar convalesces after a beating that nearly kills him, Yunior narrates: "He read *The Lord of the Rings* for what I'm estimating the millionth time, one of his greatest loves and greatest comforts since he'd first discovered it, back when he was nine and lost and lonely and his favorite librarian had said, Here, try this, and with one suggestion changed his life. Got through almost the whole trilogy, but then the line 'and out of Far Harad black men like half-trolls' and he had to stop, his head and heart hurting too much" (307). To say something is one of Oscar's greatest loves is no understatement; Oscar proves he is willing to die for love. In the end, something about Tolkien's world comforts Oscar, and that comfort has been with him for most of his life. Is it any wonder that he wished to follow in Tolkien's footsteps?

If we see Oscar's character and Tolkien's magnum opus as working together as one unit in *Oscar Wao*, we come to understand Oscar's life and therefore Yunior's narrative in the light of eucatastrophe. The deep structure of hope that runs throughout *The Lord of the Rings* may also run through *Oscar Wao*. In the footnote regarding Morgoth's bane, the final sentence reads: "They shall die without hope, cursing both life and death" (5). Though a curse is the undercurrent of Yunior's entire narrative, he is bound and determined not to let the forces of evil—those very forces that resulted in Oscar's death—be victorious by crushing all semblance of hope. Despite Yunior's contention that Trujillo's evil was somehow more potent than Sauron's, he nevertheless quotes Tolkien a second time in an uncontextualized footnote (footnote twenty). Yunior selects the passage that describes the moment of Sauron's final defeat: "And as the Captains gazed south to the Land of Mordor, it seemed to them that, black against the pall of cloud, there rose a huge shape of shadow, impenetrable, lighting-crowned, filling all the sky. Enormous it reared above the world, and stretched out towards them a vast threatening hand, terrible but impotent; for even as it leaned over them, a great wind took it, and it was blown away, and passed; and then a hush fell" (156). Yunior's avidity for apocalyptic texts also values the inherent hope or eucatastrophe that lay within those intertexts. Reading *Oscar Wao* in this light makes us consider the deep structure of hope in the novel's resolution—not only the hope that rests on the happiness Oscar experiences in his final hours with Ybon but also the hope that is the promise of Oscar's niece, Isis. Yunior's hope, admittedly a hope he barely manages to cling to, is that Isis will be able to put the fukú curse—her family's curse—behind her. Yunior muses, "And maybe, just maybe, if she's smart and as brave as I'm expecting she'll be, she'll take all we've done and all we've learned and add her own insights and she'll put an end to it. That is what, on my best days, I hope. What I dream" (332). As the Watcher, Yunior has seen enough to make him doubt that he will ever see his hopes and dreams come to fruition. But he nevertheless recognizes the deep structure of hope within Oscar's narrative.

In this story of a nerd's struggle for love that includes intertexts of African slaves' history, along with the speculative works of fiction by Jack Kirby and J. R. R. Tolkien, Díaz creates a novel unlike anything in the Latino/a literary tradition. Even the name "Oscar Wao," a corruption of Oscar Wilde, is yet another intertext, a nickname given to Oscar by his friends who erroneously think his Halloween costume is Oscar Wilde when in fact it is a Doctor Who costume. In fact, Díaz's first novel is highly intertextual thanks to a narrator that seemingly has an encyclopedic knowledge of comics, science fiction and fantasy, and apocalyptic and dystopic literature. He shows how intertexts can be used not merely as a postmodernist device that self-reflexively calls attention to itself but also as a means of providing significant layers of meaning to the narrative proper, even at the expense of a reader's smooth engagement with the novel. Because Díaz effectively levels discursive hierarchies, "the novel seems impossible to fit into any one genre."[45] Díaz makes few concessions, placing the onus of working through the intertextual material (some often obscure) on his readership. *Oscar Wao* reflects the developing nature of Latino/a literature in the twenty-first century and "offers us a model for a kind of literature that can sidestep the binary partition of authentic/inauthentic by loosening the exclusionary practices that insist on impermeable barriers between cultures and ethnicities."[46] For decades, Latino/a writers have consistently shaped their narratives to conform to a particular structure with a readership unwilling to deal with narrative challenges of language, structure, or content. Díaz makes it evident in his expansive novel that his works can engage with a wide array of human cultural production. The message is clear. If a reader does not understand a particular intertext, it is now up to the reader to make sense of it. Díaz's most valuable contribution to American literature: he has changed how readers think of a "Latino/a" novel with *Oscar Wao*.

CHAPTER 3

This Is How You Lose Her
(2012)

Five years after the publication of *The Brief Wondrous Life of Oscar Wao*, Díaz followed up his successful novel with a second collection of stories, titled *This Is How You Lose Her*. Unlike *Drown*, where Yunior is not clearly linked to several of the stories, every story in *This Is How You Lose Her* is in some way connected to him. Comprising nine stories, *This Is How* allowed Díaz to return to the love relationships that have shaped Yunior's life. *Drown* magnifies the inability of young men to express deep-felt emotions. *Oscar Wao* brings together Yunior's love for Oscar with the at times outrageous history of the Dominican Republic and its people. *This Is How* is all about Yunior even in a story such as "Otravida, Otravez," a story narrated by Ramón's lover, Yasmin. More than the previous two volumes, *This Is How* shows the arc of Yunior's emotional development and in many ways provides insight to what drives Yunior's capacity for and expression of love. While many of the stories collected in the volume appeared in earlier incarnations in literary magazines such as the *New Yorker*, *Glimmer Train*, and *Story* (seven of the nine stories are previously published), the power of reading them together as a unit resonates in a way that doesn't happen when reading any of the stories singly. This is Yunior's world, and he is more introspective and vulnerable than ever before. That Díaz was nominated for many high-

profile literary awards for *This Is How*, despite the fact that many
of the stories were previously published, speaks to the power of the
volume as a self-contained vivisection of the human heart. As with
Drown, I've partitioned the stories of *This Is How* according to shared
characteristics rather than examining them in the order in which they
appear in the book or were first published.

"OTRAVIDA, OTRAVEZ" AND "INVIERNO"

Like "Negocios" and "Aguantando" in *Drown*, "Otravida, Otravez"
and "Invierno" locate their narratives on Yunior's father, Ramón. It
cannot be happenstance that each of these stories bears a Spanish
title, as it is Ramón's predominant language. It also nods to the Spanish language as a part of the *patria*, or fatherland. Recall the difficulties Ramón has with learning English in "Negocios." Also, these two
stories in *This Is How* (and "Miss Lora," to a small extent) give us an
understanding of why Yunior is the way he is, why he continually
falters in expressions of love. He opens the book with the line, "I'm
not a bad guy," and these two stories shed light on why Yunior might
say this in his defense.[1] It is, in effect, a preemptive strike. After his
actions and opinions in *Oscar Wao*, it is easy to see why a reader might
dislike Yunior, especially in his treatment of Oscar. *This Is How* does
the work of recuperating Yunior for readers who may have forgotten
him outside of the world he narrates in *Oscar Wao*.

"Otravida, Otravez" is the fourth story in *This Is How*, and it does
not feature Yunior as a character or narrator. A woman named Yasmin narrates the story, and it allows Díaz the opportunity to employ a
female narrator, something he does sparingly in *Oscar Wao* and not at
all in *Drown*. Here Yasmin is Ramón's lover, and she is certainly not
the only woman readers have seen him with outside of his marriage.
Recall that Yunior meets a woman named Nilda later in his life, near
the end of "Negocios." (This is not to be confused with the Nilda
who appears in the story that bears her name, but it does hint at the
possibility of mistakes being passed on from father to son.) Ramón is

often portrayed through the eyes of his son, and "Otravida, Otravez" is the only example of a woman who is in a relationship with him who narrates the story.

The story's title, translated as "Another Life, Once Again," exemplifies the overarching conflict that motivates Yunior's entire life: that his proclivity to cheat on women is not necessarily a personal quirk but rather a way of life that is patriarchal and perhaps genetic in nature. Ramón carries on several relationships in which he is the central male figure. His family back in the Dominican Republic eagerly, desperately awaits his return. In the States he has at least two relationships, and in this story we adopt Yasmin's perspective. Readers understand that Yasmin is not the woman who will spend the rest of her life with Ramón; Yunior has already revealed this fact in earlier stories. In many ways, Yasmin's relationship with Ramón is an exercise in futility, and so the reader is already in a position to gravitate emotionally to her side in the matters she reveals. She is a sympathetic figure, but Díaz does not allow for a simplistic vilification of Ramón's infidelities and shortcomings. As is true for the majority of Díaz's character narrators who tell someone else's story, Yasmin is less interested in herself than she is in the man she loves.

Yasmin paints an honest picture of Ramón. He works hard, so hard that he pushes his body to extremes in order to save enough money to purchase a house—something few immigrants, according to the story, have managed to do successfully. The story opens during a harsh East Coast winter, and the poorly insulated room struggles to keep out the cold. Gazing out at the fallen snow, Ramón feels his dislocation from his home in the Dominican Republic. Díaz invokes the traditional symbolism of winter's cold as representing death when Ramón speaks of a man's death: "We had a man die today at the bread factory. . . . Este tipo fell from the rafters. Héctor found him between the conveyors" (52). In its many guises, life manifests throughout Yasmin's story—from Ramón's thoughts of the man who died, to the life Ramón had before he met Yasmin, to her possible life with Ramón, to her job at a hospital where people struggle to make it to the next day. The story speaks of those things that remind us of being alive, if not happy, such as the moment when Ramón and Yasmin embrace under their covers in order to keep out the cold with only the heat generated by their bodies to keep them warm.

Yasmin knows that Ramón and Virta are married and that he has a son. Díaz, through Yasmin, also reveals that Ramón had another son, named Enriquillo, who died. "How long did you mourn for your son?" Yasmin asks. "I mourned him a long time. I am still missing him," he replies (66). This moment is the first mention of Enriquillo in all of Díaz's stories concerning Yunior. For this one instance, because Yunior is neither a character nor the narrator of this story, readers know something about Yunior's life that even Yunior doesn't know. Yasmin serves to give us another perspective on the De Las Casas family. She is able to piece their story together through what Ramón mentions as well as the letters Virta continually sends. Those letters haunt them both, imploring him to remember his wife and children in their time of need. "*Please, please, mi querido husband, tell me what it is. How long did it take before your wife stopped mattering?*" she writes in one letter (59). Yasmin verifies that there are approximately eight years' worth of letters from Virta, which suggests that the time for his return is at hand. Recall that Yunior claims his father returned for them when he was around nine years old and that he was gone for approximately five years. Thus, Yasmin is narrating the events that will ultimately be the last she shares with Ramón before he returns to bring his wife and children to the States.

"Otravida, Otravez" traces the shapes of infidelity and resists the idea that there are neat categories that delineate the cheater, the cheated on, and the cheated with. When the story opens, Yasmin is the "other woman," but by the story's end we know that Ramón has returned to Virta, if only temporarily, and that Yasmin is really just one in a succession of women in Ramón's life. Ramón's inability to remain in a monogamous relationship may have nothing to do with his ability to feel true emotions and love for the women he is with at any given time. Rather, the cultural scripts by which he abides diminish his masculinity if he *does* remain monogamous, as Oscar and Yunior reveal in *Oscar Wao*. Ramón's work ethic is tied explicitly to the notion that the man needs to own his home, signaling his transition from immigrant guest to homeowner. Indeed, Ana María Manzanas Calvo sees the story as portraying "Dominican American migrants . . . as the recipients of a particular kind of hospitality that entails close observation akin to convalescent hospitality."[2] If Ramón can purchase a house, even one that is in dire need of repair, he is no longer an immigrant excluded because of his transient state. This fact makes Yasmin's liminality all the more poignant.

But Yasmin also focuses on how hard it is to be an immigrant *and* a woman. Most girls recently arrived, such as Samantha, are unable to continue the strenuous work amid harsh conditions and either quit the job or return to the Dominican Republic. Like Ramón, Ana Iris has left her children in order to work and save enough money to bring them to the States. It is a struggle to survive, but as Yasmin states:

> Here there are calamities without end—but sometimes I can clearly
> see us in the future, and it is good. We will live in his house and I will
> cook for him and when he leaves food out on the counter I will call
> him a zángano. I can see myself watching him shave every morning.
> And at other times I see us in that house and see how one bright day
> (a day like this, so cold your mind shifts every time the wind does) he
> will wake up and decide it's all wrong. He will wash his face and then
> turn to me. I'm sorry, he'll say. I have to leave now. (69)

There is hope amid hardship and perseverance in the face of inevitability. Ramón spends eight years' worth of savings on a dilapidated house he lovingly calls his "niño," or son. But owning a house, often a symbol of familial stability, flies in the face of Ramón's wanderlust, yet he cannot keep from aspiring to such milestones of success. He desires the house because it signifies success for him personally, rather than devotion to his family. Yasmin labors in a hospital laundering sheets stained with infectious diseases such as HIV. The fact that he might leave her at any moment looms over her relationship with Ramón. And by the end of the story, Yasmin is pregnant, with the prospect that Ramón must finally return to his children and his wife. Yasmin's realization comes when Ana Iris reveals that she can no longer stay separated from her children. Either she must return to them or she must bring them to her. Yasmin, herself carrying her first child, sitting in the middle of a park that brings such pleasure to the many children who frequent it, now understands that Ramón will leave her when he reads Virta's most recent letter that has just arrived.

In "Invierno," the title of which translates as "winter," Yunior narrates the first weeks after his father brings his family to New Jersey. Here Ramón does not have the house mentioned in "Otravida, Otravez"; instead he has a rented apartment for his family. There are several gaps in the storytelling that make a reader wonder. Does Ramón still have his house? He most certainly is still engaged in his extramarital affairs, as we see in several of the stories from Drown. Just as in "Fiesta, 1980," Yunior and Ramón are at odds because they don't know each other. Moreover, Ramón forbids his wife and children from leaving the apartment. Yunior is in a new world, a snowglobe existence where his education comes from children's animation and Sesame Street. He struggles to understand his father and often relies on Rafa to instruct him on how he ought to engage his father. As Yunior notes, "A father is a hard thing to compass" (125).

The metaphor of the compass is apt, and it speaks to the unseen sway Ramón has over his sons, whether by his absence or his dominating presence. Throughout Yunior's life he is the rotating compass needle that seeks a magnetic, or, in this case, a moral pole. Rafa is a younger version of Ramón, and Yunior often looks to his older brother for guidance as a son would a father. With these two older men to guide Yunior through his delicate, sensitive youth, it is no wonder that he patterns much of his promiscuity after them. On the other hand, Yunior is like his male role models in that he has moments of acute emotion but often dismisses them because he has no outlet for such feelings. This inability to express heartfelt emotions that contravene macho personas is a characteristic of most of Díaz's male narrators.

"Invierno" once again highlights the lack of communication between Yunior and Ramón. At one point in the story, Ramón insists that Yunior get a haircut. But Ramón instructs the barber to shave Yunior's head. Yunior remarks, "I watched the clippers plow through my hair, watched my scalp appear, tender and defenseless. One of the old men in the waiting area snorted and held his paper higher. I was sick to my stomach; I didn't want him to shave it but what could I have said to my father? I didn't have the words" (128). The haircut is but one example of the disconnect between father and son, and it punctuates the lack of love between the two of them. And when Ramón does attempt to communicate with Yunior in the story, it is often about women: "Do you like negras? my father asked. I turned my head to look at the women we had just passed. I turned back and realized that he was waiting for an answer, that he wanted to know, and while I wanted to blurt that I didn't like girls in any denomination, I said instead, Oh yes, and he smiled. They're beautiful, he said, and lit a cigarette. They'll take care of you better than anyone" (128–29). At this moment, Yunior again reveals how difficult it is for him to say what is on his mind, to tell his father his thoughts on the situation. Just as he has no influence on the kind of haircut he receives, he figuratively has no voice when speaking to his father. Instead, Yunior tells his father what he thinks his father wants to hear.

At other times in "Invierno," Yunior outright defies his father. He sneaks out of the apartment and plays in the snow with other children, "American" children from the apartment complex. When Yunior sees them, not for the first time, he cannot resist following them outside, leaving Rafa in disbelief. "Wait up! . . . I want to play with you," Yunior shouts to the children, who cannot understand his Spanish (132).

Still, it is an extraordinary experience for Yunior. Though it is a small act in context, the act of defying his father is a significant indication of Yunior's future. Unlike Rafa, Yunior doesn't have to be the same kind of man his father is. Instead, he can follow his instinct when it suits him, though the pressures of being a Dominican macho are always at work in Yunior's life, whether he likes it or not.

Because Ramón essentially has his family under house arrest, it is no wonder that they begin to feel the effects of being trapped in the apartment. Not long after Yunior ventures out to play in the snow, his mother also finds herself leaving the apartment—especially after a particularly embarrassing episode where Ramón invites his male friends over and she waits on them hand and foot. The United States has changed them all. The change in location has allowed Ramón to get away with things Virta would never allow in the Dominican Republic. Rafa obeys his father like he's never done before. Ramón has used the novelty of the United States to keep his family in check for as long as he can, but it is only a matter of time before his domineering control of his family ends.

The final scene occurs during a severe winter storm; Virta goes out into the storm while Ramón is at work and the boys are in bed. Rafa and Yunior bundle up and go out of the apartment and into the storm, where they find their mother about to cross Westminster. The ground is slick with snow and ice, and the three of them surge ahead into the storm. "I'm not good at walking on this vaina," she admits. "I'm real good," Yunior answers, "Just hold on to me" (144). And the three of them march in a straight line, and, for the first time, get a look at their new home. "Invierno" ends with a preview of what their life will be in years to come. Soon enough Ramón will no longer be with them, and in time Rafa, too, will be gone. Virta's resolve is indicated in how she braves the United States in the midst of a severe winter storm. And Yunior, for all of his shortcomings past and future, will support his mother emotionally through future heartaches and pains.

In "Otravida, Otravez" and "Invierno," the winter of Ramón's discontent is on full display. He is as complicated a figure as his son, and these stories outline the type of patrimony the father leaves for the son—a code of masculinity and discipline that informs him as a father, a husband, and lover. Never again does Ramón appear in any of the stories in *This Is How*, but his presence looms over the lives of his sons in ways that he may never have anticipated. His influence holds particular sway over Rafa, and the next group of stories to be discussed explores Yunior's older brother and his tortured relationships with women and his family.

"NILDA," "THE PURA PRINCIPLE," AND "MISS LORA"

These three stories feature Yunior's brother Rafa in some significant way, and they logically follow Ramón's stories because, in Ramón absence, Rafa has become the head of the household and thus becomes a father figure to Yunior. There is also a specific woman at the heart of each of these stories, and each of them shapes Yunior's understanding of women as well as his male family members. Like in many of Díaz's other stories, Yunior's narration informs his development as a man as well as a character. In addition, these stories make a point of emphasizing the lead-up to Rafa's death from what appears to be leukemia. Yunior ruminates on his brother's death, now without the two men who have, directly or indirectly, influenced his life and ability to connect emotionally with women. In many ways Yunior undergoes the process of emotional education in these three stories both as an observer of his older brother's struggles with life and love and as a young man learning to grapple with his passions.

"Nilda" is the second story in *This Is How*, and it features Yunior as a narrator. Because Yunior typically narrates in the past tense, there is always the impression that he is reflecting on how certain events turned out rather than just recounting stories from his youth. Yunior's narration is a reminder that, when considering all of the Yunior stories holistically, we are seeing snapshots of him at crucial moments in

his life. In such times, Yunior is often naïve or immature when compared to the older, ostensibly wiser man who is narrating the stories.
Unsavory characteristics that make Yunior such a vulnerable, flawed
character—such as his objectification of women—are further illuminated the more stories he narrates. In "Nilda," it is as if Yunior has
been reminded recently of his brother's one-time girlfriend, and the
flood of memories sweeps him into the rapids of narrative and readers
are swept away with him, as if someone had asked him if he knew
Nilda and he replied, "Nilda was my brother's girlfriend" (29).

Rafa often keeps Nilda at arm's length, sneaking her into the basement and having sex with her while Yunior remains quiet on his side
of the basement. Yunior recalls, "Rafa didn't make no noise, just a low
something that resembled breathing. Nilda was the one. She seems to
be trying to hold back from crying the whole time. It was crazy hearing her like that. The Nilda I'd grown up with was one of the quietest
girls you'd ever meet. She let her hair wall away her face and read *The
New Mutants*, and the only time she looked straight at anything was
when she looked out a window" (29). That Yunior cannot see Nilda
in that context, that it was "crazy hearing her like that," emphasizes
that he is in a transitional period in his life. Not long before, "before
she'd gotten that chest, before that slash of black hair had gone from
something to pull on the bus to something to stroke in the dark" (29),
Nilda and Yunior had at least *The New Mutants* in common. But like
Beli in *Oscar Wao*, puberty suddenly changes Nilda into a different
person. Yunior describes the postpubescent Nilda as "the new Nilda,"
and it is not insignificant that once again Yunior draws upon a comic
book intertext to underscore his point. In this case, he invokes the
X-Men spinoff of youths who suddenly find themselves changed,
and marginalized, as a result of some physical change in their bodies.
Nilda has crossed over into the sexual domain with Rafa, and Yunior
adopts his watcher role (i.e., Uatu) in prepubescence.

Often in *Oscar Wao* Yunior takes the stance that Oscar is the
"ghetto nerd at the end of the world," that Oscar is the mutant, mar-

ginalized in every social group in which he finds himself. But over the course of Yunior's stories he reveals that he, too, is a ghetto nerd— a mutant who must hide his superhuman abilities in order to avoid social ostracization. At fourteen Yunior was "reading *Dhalgren* for the second time," and "had an IQ that would have broken you in two but I would have traded it in for a halfway decent face in a second" (31). In a less exaggerated way, Yunior's dilemma of a high IQ, his affinity for literature (both literary and popular), and his preoccupation with his looks is quite similar to Oscar's. Oscar's entire life is a struggle to reconcile his nerd tendencies with the expectations of his culture— a struggle for which he willingly sacrifices his life. In contrast, Yunior has the gift of passing that allows him to suppress his bookish characteristics and revel in the codes of machismo when necessary.

If Rafa and Yunior reside in opposite spheres, Nilda is the one who can move between the two of them. She visits on Thursdays, what Yunior calls "comic-book day," but Nilda waits for Rafa to come home. Yunior is aware of Rafa's capacity to use women, but he also has affection for Nilda: "I wanted to warn her, tell her he was a monster, but she was already headed for him at the speed of light" (33). Rafa is at the height of his machismo powers. His body is "something out of a Frazetta drawing" and "even the whitegirls knew about my overmuscled about-to-be-a-senior brother and were impressed" (33, 34). But Yunior also notes the onset of what will prove to be Rafa's fatal battle with cancer: "Rafa was tired all the time and pale: this had happened in a matter of days" (35). Just as his father Ramón had finally left, what Yunior calls the "Last Great Absence," Rafa will soon be gone as well.

Yunior cannot understand why Rafa treats Nilda as indifferently as he does. On the night she reveals her plans for the future, the hopeful possibilities in the face of her impoverished environment, her ruminations profoundly affect Yunior. For him, her plans are an indication of the love she has for Rafa. Nilda's monologue moves Yunior, yet Rafa remains impassive: "When she finished he didn't even say wow. I wanted to kill myself with embarrassment. About a half hour later she got up and dressed. She couldn't see me or she would have known that I thought she was beautiful" (38). Yunior's narrative quakes in incredulity and indignation at Rafa's treatment of Nilda. Within two years, Rafa will be gone.

Both Yunior and Nilda struggle after Rafa's death. Upon reflection, Yunior cannot understand how a relationship that lasted just one summer looms so large in his memory. He then reveals the impetus for his story. His tense changes to the present and he finds that he and Nilda are at the same laundromat all these years later. Their sparse conversation turns, naturally, to Rafa. "I miss him sometimes," Yunior admits. As they leave for the old neighborhood, Yunior thinks of Nilda, "We could do anything. We could marry. We could drive off to the West Coast. We could start over. It's all possible but neither of us speaks for a long time and the moment closes and we're back in the world we've always known" (42). Just at the moment when he might change their lives forever, Yunior finds himself mute.

"Nilda" reveals how the De Las Casas brothers emotionally engage the world in different ways. Nilda herself proves to be the nexus where the brothers meet and distinguish themselves on an emotional level. Though Yunior at times has very strong feelings for Nilda, the story is not about her, despite its title. But as in many of the stories Yunior narrates, Nilda is an outsider figure for whom he feels compassion and empathy. She allows him the opportunity to reassess not only himself but his brother as well.

Yunior's most intense examination of his relationship with this brother comes in the story "The Pura Principle." The sixth story of the collection, "The Pura Principle" uncovers the final months of Rafa's life as he struggles with cancer as well as the brothers' relationship with one another. Though there has always been the sense of a sibling rivalry in many of the stories in which Yunior and Rafa appear, that fraternal antagonism only increases during Rafa's terminal illness. There is none of the stereotypical mending of proverbial fences as

Rafa approaches his death. Instead, Rafa becomes more incorrigible as his time grows short. The ever-present tension between the brothers now becomes untenable. "No way of wrapping it pretty or pretending otherwise," Yunior notes of the final months of Rafa's life (91).

The reliable triad of the brothers and their mother creates the foundation for the family dynamic. It is the configuration of the family unit that has served as the basis of most of Yunior's life experiences. At times when his father is a major figure in Yunior's life the family becomes unstable. It is as if a new member of a well-practiced team is introduced; the inclusion of the new member destabilizes comfortable tendencies. In "The Pura Principle," it is not Ramón who destabilizes the family but the last girlfriend of Rafa's life, Pura. She disrupts an already volatile situation, and the story encapsulates Pura's intrusion into what should be the family's private suffering.

Yunior describes his detachment from the pain of Rafa's struggle with cancer with bravado typical for him as a character. He glosses over his inability at the age of seventeen to face the cruel reality that Rafa would soon die, noting, "I wouldn't have wanted to talk about it. . . . The few times my boys at school tried to bring it up, I told them to mind their own fucking business. To get out of my face" (90). That the Yunior who is now narrating the story, ostensibly many years since the time in question, can face the pain associated with that time reveals the depth of his emotional development.

To his credit, Yunior is not the only family member unable to bear the inevitable demise of the firstborn De Las Casas son. Yunior uses biting sarcasm to describe his mother's desperate embrace of religion: "I think she would have nailed herself to a cross if she'd had one handy" (91). A group of women Yunior deridingly calls "The Four Horsefaces of the Apocalypse" (91) lends emotional and spiritual support to his mother, and he finds this intrusion into the family as an annoyance. They are a group of misfits, yet they "were my mother's only friends—even our relatives had gotten scarce after year two," Yunior notes.

For his entire life up to that moment, in the stories Díaz writes of the two brothers, Yunior has been overshadowed by Rafa. Here Rafa's imminent death obliterates Yunior's development at this crucial moment—just before he turns eighteen—and dominates every aspect of Yunior's and his mother's lives. What should be a time of healing, a time of closure, ends up as a further rupture of the family tissue that, for as long as Yunior remembers, has always been damaged. And Rafa is determined to go out on his terms, detaching himself from any emotional concerns. As Yunior states, "But of all of us Rafa took the cake. When he'd come home from the hospital this second go-round, he fronted like nothing had happened. Which was kinda nuts, considering that half the time he didn't know where the fuck he was because of what the radiation had done to his brain and the other half he was too tired even to fart" (93).

Despite the ravages of the chemo on Rafa's body, he goes about his life in his own, volatile way. He gets into vicious fights, womanizes according to his "papi chulo" scripts, and completely disregards the admonitions of Yunior and his mother. The emotional vacuum in their lives prevents any sort of honest communication. In the momentary quiescence before Pura appears, Yunior recalls: "I sat with him sometimes when the Mets were playing, and he wouldn't say a word about how he was feeling, what he was expecting to happen. It was only when he was in bed, dizzy or nauseous, that I'd hear him groaning: What the hell is happening? What do I do? What do I do?" (96). Cancer compels Rafa to be vulnerable, to allow his mother to take care of him, to stop being so hard on his body, to start showing his brother love before he runs out of time. But Rafa has never been taught how to acknowledge and handle his emotions. His uncertainty, and Yunior's as well, comes from a lack of emotional preparedness.

Rafa shocks Yunior by getting a job at an arts and crafts store named the Yarn Barn. Yunior sees this as an incomprehensible move by his brother. Rafa takes a kind of pride in his work, but his illness forces him to quit the job. Yunior can see this is an odd behavior for

Rafa, and in many ways he is not that surprised that Rafa ultimately marries the woman who finds him collapsed in an aisle of the Yarn Barn. Her name is Pura Adames, and her arrival allows for Rafa's movement through the final stage of his life.

Ironically, in the midst of Rafa's death spiral, Pura brings vitality to the family dynamic, and, most importantly, disrupts Yunior's mother's expectations for how her eldest son will meet his death. That is to say, Pura dislodges Rafa's mother's place and bolsters him in his final moments. Pura embodies the Dominican identity, "*Dominican* Dominican," as Yunior recounts (100). She is ignorant of American culture and mostly oblivious to the insults Rafa's mother hurls at her. In addition, Pura is honest to a fault. "She'd talk your ear off if you let her, and was way too honest: within a week she'd told us her whole life story. How her father had died when she was young; how for an undisclosed sum her mother had married her off at thirteen to a stingy fifty-year-old," and so on. Not only does Pura magnify for the reader the family's inability to communicate, she is a natural antagonist to Rafa's mother, who takes every opportunity to express her extreme displeasure with Pura.

This emotional dynamic leads to a rift between Rafa and his mother, and Yunior can hardly believe it. "My mother couldn't resist my brother. Not ever. No matter what the fuck he pulled—and my brother pulled a lot of shit—she was always a hundred percent on his side, as only a Latin mom can be with her querido oldest hijo. If he'd come home one day and said, Hey, Ma, I exterminated half the planet, I'm sure she would have defended his ass: Well, hijo, we were overpopulated" (107). Pura's introduction has taken a family that is indifferent to the encroaching death of one of its members and ignites suppressed emotions. She enables Rafa to return to his former self, even if it is only temporarily. The moment she leaves Rafa and his family, Yunior reveals the return to the lack of communication in the family: "He didn't say a thing about Pura. Didn't talk much about anything. . . . I tried to stay out of the way. . . . Every now and then when me and Rafa were alone and the game was on I tried to talk to him, but he never said nothing back" (117–18). The story's culminating scene best exemplifies their refusal to talk to one another. Seemingly out of nowhere, Yunior is struck in the face by a Yale padlock. It does not take him long to understand who launched it. Fulfilling a promise made earlier in the story, Rafa says, "Didn't I tell you I was going to fix you? Didn't I?" (118).

In what will be the final moments between brothers, moments that ought to be cherished, Rafa follows through on the only scripts he has known his entire life—those of violence toward his brother. Because readers are never privy to the narration that reveals Rafa's perspective or intent, Rafa remains something like a cipher—an embodied code of masculinity, fraternal love, and sexual passion. If one reads "The Pura Principle" as a stand-alone story, it doesn't seem to have the same sort of impact that it would make on a reader with a more fully developed understanding of the Yunior-Rafa dyad. Within "The Pura Principle" little changes in Rafa's character, or in Yunior's for that matter. The change occurs from story to story. As the changes are so small within stories such as this one, there is a frustrating quality to Rafa's recalcitrance. The story informs Yunior's character as it gives the knowing reader a glimpse into what has helped shape Yunior's sense of self.

As a character in development, Yunior stands out in further relief when he narrates the story "Miss Lora." The penultimate story in the collection, "Miss Lora" places the overwhelming force Rafa has on his brother alongside the sexual act as a transition from boyhood to manhood. Disturbingly, the story revolves around an act of rape. Díaz exposes the hypocrisy and double standards society at large maintains regarding an underage boy having a sexual relationship with an adult woman. Further, Miss Lora is much older than Yunior. As is characteristic of stories about Yunior's development, his decision-making process is completely influenced by the older men in his life. In this case, both of these men—Rafa and Ramón—are gone. The story, divided into fifteen vignettes, begins with Yunior's reflection of his brother: "Years later you wonder if it hadn't been for your brother would you have done it?" (149).

The first section is a remembrance of what amounts to Rafa's approval of Miss Lora. Because his approval is based solely on the sexual act, Rafa simply sees Miss Lora as a woman to be fucked, as yet another sexual conquest. But as Yunior sees it, if Rafa was willing to fuck Miss Lora, then doing so was good enough for Yunior. The memory of his older brother causes Yunior to dwell on the loss that he feels. What's more, two issues he cannot seem to come to terms with devastate Yunior. On the one hand, he truly misses his brother. On the other hand, Rafa was a terrible brother. Yunior states, "Your brother. Dead nearly a year and sometimes you still feel a fulgurating sadness over it even though he really was a super asshole in the end. He didn't die easy at all. Those last months he just steady kept trying to run away" (149). Although his brother is gone, Yunior feels his presence in his absence, particularly when it comes to Miss Lora. It is as if Yunior seeks to live out what his brother could not do before he died. And most painful of all is that his brother refused to talk to him as the end came. The specter of Rafa hovers over the entire story even though Yunior mentions him in only four of the fifteen sections. Yunior's reflection of his older brother opens the story as if it is the impetus for his relationship with Miss Lora. And after the second section comes to a close, Yunior concentrates on Miss Lora until section nine. Here Yunior sees himself as yet another in a line of womanizers: "Both your father and your brother were some sucios. Shit, your father used to take you on his pussy runs, leave you in the car while he ran up into cribs to bone his girlfriends. Your brother was no better, bedding girls in the bed next to yours. Sucios of the worst kind and now it's official: You are one, too. You had hoped the gene missed you, skipped a generation, but clearly you're kidding yourself" (161). Yunior makes an excuse for his behavior. In his rationalization, his failing is genetic. It is a legacy that he must accept. Though he does not say it, it's not unlike a family curse, a fukú, the kind he mentions in *The Brief Wondrous Life of Oscar Wao.*

Yunior also has a girlfriend named Paloma. He fell in love with her at the age of sixteen. As the events in the story take place in 1985, Yunior is completely awash in narratives that presage nuclear destruction. That Paloma fails to feel the fear of the dawning apocalypse only serves to reinforce Yunior's private struggles with his dread of the future. Paloma's future stretches out before her in a clear, uncomplicated path that takes her from high school to college and beyond. She refuses to have sex with Yunior because she recognizes the potential for getting pregnant. Having a child would undoubtedly complicate her desire to go to college. As Yunior states, "Paloma was convinced that if she made any mistakes in the next two years, any mistakes at all, she would be stuck in that family of hers forever. That was her nightmare" (151–52). While both Yunior and Paloma consider their future, Yunior's fears are much more existential. Paloma has a clear ability to see consequences of actions. Yunior fears not just the end of his world as Paloma would see it; he fears a literal end of the world courtesy of nuclear proliferation and mutually assured destruction. Thus, narratives that depict the end of the world by human hands fascinate Yunior. And when he doesn't find this common interest in Paloma, he seeks someone, anyone, who would listen. With a mutual interest in apocalyptic narratives, Yunior and Miss Lora begin to spend more and more time together. If we take Yunior at his word, his initial attraction to Miss Lora is not based on her physical attributes. Or at least, it is not the physical characteristics to which he or his brother or his father would find himself attracted. And though he may not realize it at the time, this distinguishes Yunior from either his brother or his father.

The more stories one reads about Yunior, the more one gets the feeling that he doesn't want to be like his brother or father. In many ways, it is the source of his conflict. Regarding Miss Lora, he notes, "Miss Lora wasn't nothing exciting. There were about a thousand viejas in the neighborhood way hotter, like Mrs. del Orbe, whom your brother had fucked silly until her husband found out and moved the whole family away. Miss Lora was too skinny. Had no hips whatsoever. No breasts, either, no ass, even her hair failed to make the grade. She had her eyes, sure, but what she was most famous for in the neighborhood were her muscles" (153–54). Not only is Miss Lora an anomaly in the neighborhood for not having children at her age, she has the physique of a bodybuilder. Yunior finds her body attractive. His desire for Miss Lora and his fear of imminent destruction lead him to a physical relationship with an older woman.

Yunior has recurring dreams of nuclear war and atomic fallout. During his dreams, Yunior bites his tongue until it bleeds. As a sixteen-year-old, Yunior is very aware of his body. He runs to get into better shape and hopes it may help with his acne. He lifts weights and watches the results as young bodybuilders do. Interestingly, although Paloma is Yunior's ostensible girlfriend in the story, he never describes her body. That is to say, her body does not drive his behavior the way other women in other stories have done, such as Nilda, Flaca, or Alma. Miss Lora's body, which disgusts Paloma, takes center stage in the story. The difference between Miss Lora and Paloma comes to the fore in the scene that has Miss Lora giving Yunior a blowjob: "You try to think of Paloma, so exhausted that every morning she falls asleep on the ride to school. Paloma, who still found the energy to help you study for your SAT. Paloma, who didn't give you any ass because she was terrified that if she got pregnant she wouldn't abort it out of love for you and then her life would be over. You're trying to think of her but what you're doing is holding Miss Lora's tresses like reins and urging her head to keep this wonderful rhythm" (160). Díaz highlights the difference between the two women in this scene. Paloma is a strong female character, a character who knows exactly the topography of the terrain of her life. She unerringly understands what it means to have a baby in high school, and thus, she understands the implications of having sex at that age. Yunior, on the other hand, in the tradition of his father and brother, can have sex indiscriminately with any women he chooses without fearing the end of his life as he knows it. Yunior's hypothetical end-of-the-world scenario, though very much a possibility in the mid-1980s, is far from the actuality of having a child out of wedlock while still in one's teens. Indeed, in another moment in the story, Yunior admits that he doesn't have a condom. Miss Lora doesn't let that prevent them from consummating their relationship. As she is most likely past her childbearing years, Miss Lora does not exercise the same sort of caution Paloma does. Miss Lora can't ruin her life. Or as Yunior's mother might say, it cannot be ruined further.

As Yunior's relationship with Miss Lora escalates, as he finds himself at her apartment every day, he finds that his nightmares continue unabated. He wonders, "It should be the greatest thing, so why are your dreams worse? Why is there more blood in the sink in the morning?" (163). In time he finds out more about Miss Lora's background, and she often attempts to get Yunior to talk about Rafa and, specifically, his death. Yunior cannot bring himself to talk about it, and the lingering grief distracts his mother from attending to her living son, completely unaware of the relationship he is having with Miss Lora. By the time Yunior is a senior in high school Miss Lora takes a job at his school, adding another layer of illegality to their relationship, but neither Yunior nor Miss Lora brings the relationship to an end. It is not until Yunior graduates from high school, and even after his senior year at Rutgers, that he begins to come to terms with his relationship with Miss Lora. As he finally confesses his secret of the relationship he had with Miss Lora, his girlfriend puts it plainly: "They should arrest that crazy bitch" (170).

In the final section of the story, Miss Lora appears at Yunior's graduation at Rutgers. After some time, once Yunior and his girlfriend are over, Yunior looks for Miss Lora again. He searches for her on the internet, and later when he goes to the Dominican Republic, he asks about her as he shows people a picture of the two of them together. Miss Lora played such a prominent role in Yunior's sense of sexual self that he can never get rid of her, despite his efforts. Among all of his relationships with women, Miss Lora looms large.

Considering the story in light of others that feature Yunior, the relationship he had at the age of sixteen with an older woman allows insight into much of his development as a character. Their relationship forbidden and secret but there is also an unexpected tenderness and understanding in it. It is this contradiction that makes the story so insightful for understanding Yunior as a character. It also underscores Díaz's technique for placing young Latino men in emotionally difficult circumstances where the traditional scripts that a man must follow in Latino culture in America and the Dominican Republic are insufficient. The more we read about Yunior's development as a man vis-à-vis his romantic relationships, the more we wonder how he is supposed to negotiate these inflexible identity positions, in which he is expected to disregard genuine emotional engagement with people. These expectations are made manifest in the figures of his brother and his father. They set the bar of masculinity for Yunior. But quite often in his stories Díaz provides the window into the young Latino man's emotional character and quality. Yunior mourns the loss of his older brother, but he also regrets their inability to say what they truly feel for one another. Similarly, Yunior is never able to come to terms, emotionally, with his father. And though Yunior is a highly sensitive person who consistently ruminates on his feelings, he often withholds this emotional content from the women he dates and occasionally loves. In the next three stories, the influences that have shaped Yunior's sense of self, such as his brother, his father, and Miss Lora, now inform our understanding of his relationships later in life.

"THE SUN, THE MOON, THE STARS," "ALMA," AND "FLACA"

Unlike the stories that feature Yunior as a prominent character or narrator under the shadow of Rafa or Ramón, "The Sun, the Moon, the Stars" exposes Yunior's frustrations in relationships and with women.

Here there is no specter of his brother looming in the recesses of
Yunior's memory. There are no deliberate reconstructions of what
might have been if Ramón had only been more of a devoted father to
his children and husband to his wife. These other stories reveal that
Yunior's predilection for the self-destruction of otherwise stable relationships is a byproduct of the male influences in the early years of
his life. Again, the difference in readership affects Yunior's reception.
Reading each of these three stories without the benefit of the deeper
knowledge of how Yunior came to be what he is casts him in a much
more disagreeable light. Yunior's complexity is revealed as the stories
cohere, and the process of knowing Yunior echoes the idea that he is
much misunderstood. For his part, Yunior seems to think his genetics
are his destiny, that because his father and brother thought little of
stable relationships, be they with sexual partners or family members,
he too must live his life according to the male scripts he's seen his
entire life. The conflict between Yunior's adherence to male behavior
and his desire to fully engage the powerful emotions he feels works
to confound readers.

"The Sun, the Moon, the Stars" opens *This Is How You Lose Her*,
and its opening situates it to initiate the collection: "I'm not a bad
guy. I know how that sounds—defensive, unscrupulous—but it's true.
I'm like everybody else: weak, full of mistakes, but basically good" (3).
Though readers have every reason to distrust such a declaration by a
character narrator—those most unreliable of narrators—the prepon-
derance of the stories in which Yunior is featured vouches for the
veracity of this opening salvo. Yunior *is* weak; he *is* full of mistakes.
The knowledgeable reader takes Yunior's confession at face value. In
contrast to Yunior's position that he is "basically good" is Magdalena, another woman in a long line of them in Yunior's life. The juxtaposition is critical to understanding Yunior as an adult, as a man
come into his own. Magdalena "considers [him] a typical Dominican
man: a sucio, an asshole" (3). For Magdalena, the typical Dominican
man is a deficient creature, lacking the necessary characteristics for a

healthy relationship. When Yunior disagrees with Magdalena's position, arguing that he is good, he does not disagree with her assertion
regarding Dominican men. "I'm not like them," Yunior seems to say.
But if we take his actions without bias, he does seem to comport with
Magdalena's expectation of him.

He freely raises the issue that has compromised his relationship
with Magda: that he cheated on her "many months ago . . . with
this chick who had tons of eighties freestyle hair" (3). And after this
"smelly bone," as Yunior describes Cassandra, she writes Magda a
letter with all sorts of compromising details. After months of their
relationship functioning like a proper one, Cassandra's letter destroys
any harmony Yunior and Magda may have had at the time. "You don't
even want to hear how it went down with Magda," Yunior admits.
"Like a five-train collision." This collision is the impetus for this story,
the moment of rupture with which Yunior must contend, despite the
fact that *he* has initiated the train wreck of an affair. It is a disaster of
his own making, and Yunior is now confronted with the aftermath of
the collision.

Much of Yunior's sense of self, as well as his sense of expectation,
is ingrained in his decision-making process once Magda finds out
about his affair. With Magda hyperventilating at the news, Yunior
lays out the course of possible actions he might take: "This is when
my boys claim they would have pulled a Total Fucking Denial. Cassandra *who*? I was too sick to my stomach even to try: I sat down next
to her, grabbed her flailing arms, and said some dumb shit like You
have to listen to me, Magda. Or you won't understand" (4). Yunior's
"boys" stand in for the typical Dominican men Magda knows about
all too well. In this situation, Yunior is expected to deny all knowledge
of any affairs. But not only does Yunior refuse to deny the relationship with Cassandra, as his friends would have, he is overcome with a
sickening feeling. As he attempts to communicate with Magda, even
he knows his words are the equivalent of "some dumb shit" that will
have little potential for salving the pain of Magda's discovery.

Like Paloma in "Miss Lora," Magda is a young, smart, strong woman who knows what she wants for her life. She is a religious woman who compels Yunior to attend Catholic mass every Sunday, the student all teachers and librarians fawn over. Yunior does not make excuses for his actions. It would be easy to justify his actions by describing Magda with all her imperfections laid bare for the reader. Instead, he admits, "You couldn't think of anybody worse to screw than Magda" (5). And yet, by screwing Cassandra, he metaphorically screws Magda. Despite working hard to win back Magda's love, if not her trust, he has irreparably damaged his standing in the relationship.

Why does Yunior attempt to rebuild his relationship with Magda, as she asks him directly? "Why don't you leave me alone?" she asks Yunior. His answer again forces readers to confront this untenable position: "I told her the truth: It's because I love you, mami. I know this sounds like a load of doo-doo, but it's true: Magda's my heart. I didn't want her to leave me; I wasn't about to start looking for a girlfriend because I'd fucked up one lousy time" (6).

For the remainder of the story, Yunior alternates between the contrite penitent and stubborn macho. His vacillation mirrors Magda's oscillation between the woman she was before Yunior's affair and the woman she promises to be—a woman without Yunior in her life. Magda is buoyed by her girlfriends, "the sorest losers on the planet," Yunior calls them, and they consistently distrust Yunior's intentions ever since his affair. But he has his cadre of friends to push him in a direction that he wants to avoid. His boys want him to be the typical Dominican man and move on from Magda. When Yunior has the idea of taking Magda on a vacation, his boys tell him, "Nigger, sounds like you're wasting a whole lot of loot on some bullshit" (6). Is Yunior naïve in his expectations, in his hope that a real healing of his relationship with Magda is a possibility? The only answer here can be yes. But therein lies Yunior's complexity, that which makes him atypical compared to other Dominican men. It is not in his actions where Yunior differentiates himself from the typical sucio. Rather, the genuine difference in Yunior lies in the emotional turmoil that ebbs and flows within his perception of his experience. These vortices of pained rationalization are delivered through the process of narration. The reader is privy to Yunior's internalization of experience in a way that not even his boys can know. Throughout all of Yunior's narration the reader is a confidante, a secret sharer that enables Yunior to come to terms with the consequences of loss, of trauma, of regret, and of love. As he admits, "Deep down, where my boys don't know me, I'm an optimist. I thought, Me and her on the Island. What couldn't this cure?" (8).

Indeed, Yunior is a constant optimist. In many ways he is also a hopeless romantic. He is ever hopeful—that he will find love, that he will keep from screwing it up, that the fukú curse will come to an end. And in "The Sun, the Moon, the Stars," which recounts events that occured when Yunior is a young man, he establishes this hopefulness that may allow him one day to sidestep the patrimony of his father —what we might call "the cheater's gene." Yunior hopes that a vacation to the Island will serve as a panacea for his relationship with Magda. This sort of thinking reveals not only his naïveté but also his desire to fix something that may be irreparable.

In his retrospective narration, Yunior sees all the signs of his obtuseness. Not only is this an indication of the perspective he has gained in the interim, it highlights just how wishful he was that his act of betrayal could be forgiven. In truth, Magda is entirely capable of forgiving Yunior his single act of transgression. What she cannot forgive is the inevitability that Yunior will cheat again and again. Magda can recognize this truth even while Yunior blindly believes there is some hope that he will never again stray.

Their trip to Santo Domingo reveals just how great the emotional gulf between Yunior and Magda has become. Yunior is embarrassed at having to stay at resorts where only well-to-do tourists would spend time. Magda wants time to herself and cannot express her displeasure to Yunior. He asks her to say she loves him, and she replies,

"Yunior, please" (16). When Yunior encounters a character he calls
the Vice-President and his bodyguard named Bárbaro at a local bar,
the Vice-President advises Yunior to find another woman. The advice
Yunior receives echoes the sort he has already received from his boys:
"Why'd you tell her? . . . Why didn't you just deny it?" (18). Yunior's
actions are counterintuitive for a Dominican man.

And Yunior's penchant for the counterintuitive drives all of the
characters in the story. He wants desperately to believe that he is
not like his father or other typical Dominican men: "All of Magda's
friends say I cheated because I was Dominican, that all of us Dominican men are dogs and can't be trusted. I doubt that I can speak for
all Dominican men but I doubt they can either. From my perspective it wasn't genetics; there were reasons. Causalities" (19). Here he
reveals the driving fear that underpins all of Yunior's dalliances: Are
his actions genetic? His vociferous denial seems convincing. Across
the broad spectrum of Yunior's narratives, he is less than certain.

As their trip inexorably deteriorates and Yunior storms off, he
repeats to himself, "I'm not a bad guy. I'm not a bad guy" (22). When
he finds himself with the Vice-President and Bárbaro once more,
they drive off to see the Cave of the Jagua, "The Birthplace of the
Taínos," the Vice-President claims (24). In the darkness, staring into
the abyss, Yunior's thoughts turn to Magda, to their first encounter
while they were students at Rutgers. Yunior now realizes his relationship with Magda is at an end and cries.

In retrospective narration, Yunior recognizes the end was at that
moment on the Island. And, as proof, he mentions the letter Magda
sends him five months after their trip, detailing that she has moved
on. But as the story serves as a type of penance, Yunior cannot resist
showing the folly of his thoughts. "But I'm getting ahead of myself.
I need to finish by showing you what kind of fool I was" (25). And
he does exactly that, by recounting how his true nature, the real pro-
gramming of his genetics, is to be a naïve romantic: "I sat down next
to her. Took her hand. This can work, I said. All we have to do is try"

(25). Even while staring at the end of his relationship, Yunior is ever hopeful that, through some mysterious means, he can recapture the integrity of Madga's love for him, irrespective of the fact that her love has shattered into innumerable shards. His wishful thinking cannot repair the damage that has already been done.

Yunior continues his self-chastising tone in "Alma," which is narrated in second person. As the shortest of all of the stories in *This Is How You Lose Her*, "Alma" is an intense study of a woman who, unlike Magda, does not mince words with Yunior after he cheats on her. Alma, "who has a long tender horse neck and a big Dominican ass that seems to exist in the fourth dimension beyond jeans" (45), is an artist and a lover of comic books—a seeming perfect match for someone like Yunior, except she is not. "You are both so very different," the narrator observes (46). She is Latina but lacks a robust engagement with her heritage, although she makes more of an attempt while dating Yunior. As the brief story progresses, the narrator notes how the stark contrasts between Yunior and Alma are a positive, "it's an opposites-attract sort of thing" (47). Alma is also quite sexually aggressive by nature: "She's more adventurous in bed than any girl you've had; on your first date she asked you if you wanted to come on her tits or her face, and maybe during boy training you didn't get one of the memos but you were, like, umm, neither" (46–47).

Because Yunior's entire understanding of what it means to be a man is couched in the idea of sexual prowess and promiscuity, Alma ought to be the kind of woman that keeps Yunior from following his cheating impulses. It is an understatement to say that Alma is a straight man's porn fantasy realized. And yet, Yunior cannot remain faithful. When Alma discovers that he has cheated on her with a "beautiful freshman named Laxmi" by reading Yunior's journal, he makes a lame attempt at "prevaricating to the end" (47, 48). Yunior has been through this before and knows it is over. If he learned anything from cheating on Magda in "The Sun, the Moon, the Stars," it's that prolonging the inevitable works to no one's benefit. But he does make one last stand, basing it in his writing. "Then you look at her and smile a smile your dissembling face will remember until the day you die. Baby, you say, baby, this is part of my novel" (48). The following line, the final line, appears as its own paragraph: "This is how you lose her."

This line, of course, serves as the title for the entire collection of stories. Not only does it occupy the terminus of the story, and, thus, hold a position of privilege as a result, but its importance as the book's title resonates. In "Alma," the second-person narrator, which can only be read as Yunior, suggests that the final insult of claiming his journal confession is a work of fiction leads to the end of the relationship. In other words, he loses her not because he cheats on her but because he lies to her. It is the exact sort of denial recommended by Yunior's boys and the Vice-President in "The Sun, the Moon, the Stars." Alma may have suspected Yunior was cheating, as the narrator suggests, but to have him mention it in his journal—through his writing—is meaningful. Taken in their totality, Yunior's stories all seem to be working through traumatic experiences in his life. Or, if not trauma per se, then moments in his life that resonate and linger in Yunior's memory. As a means of coming to terms with these experiences, he writes. The process of reliving and reexamining these people, these instances through his writing allows for the possibility that Yunior may learn something of himself from these moments.

To further extend this point, we consider the narrative stance adopted in the story. All of Díaz's stories that are narrated by a second-person narrator may well be Yunior's writing projects—assignments and stories that have come to him perhaps as he has progressed through his own writing program, and, later, as a creative writing teacher. The point ought not to be missed. For example, a story like "No Face" can easily be a story written by Yunior, based on his experiences that are recounted in "Ysrael." In "Alma," Yunior adopts the position of the second-person narrator because it allows him to take a much more severe critical stance than if it were written in the first person, particularly if he is his own subject. There appears to be very little rationalization for Yunior's actions, and his tongue-in-cheek excuses come across as pathetic and puny. The most powerful use of focalization through Yunior's experience comes at the moment when he realizes that Alma knows, evidenced by her grip on his journal, when "your heart plunges through you like a fat bandit through a hangman's trap" (47). The analogy is a devastating critique of Yunior's transgression. The momentary focalization continues: "You are overwhelmed by a pelagic sadness. Sadness at being caught, at the incontrovertible knowledge that she will never forgive you." It is the only moment in which Yunior, as the second-person narrator, exposes the emotions that, at least momentarily, overwhelm Yunior the character.

In the end, however, Yunior maintains his criticism of himself through to the end of the story by revealing the embarrassing level of immaturity with which he attempts to handle the discovery of his infidelity. His journal, which contains the writings of a life lived, is rendered as "a baby's beshatted diaper" or "a recently benutted condom" (48). In essence, his writings are as useful as baby shit, as vital as the contents of a spent condom. "Alma" lays bare another instance of Yunior's cheating in which he must ultimately shoulder the blame. Amid all of the different women featured in Díaz's writings, the message that rings clearly is that nothing is ever good enough to keep Yunior from his cheater's outlook on women.

"Flaca," the middle story of *This Is How You Lose Her*, continues Díaz's use of second-person narration. Unlike "Alma," "Flaca," about Yunior's relationship with a white girl, directs Yunior's narration at Veronica (Flaca) rather than at himself. The conceit of this story is not Yunior's cheating but rather the distance between their respective cultures. At one point Yunior muses, "Maybe five thousand years ago we were together." Flaca responds, "Five thousand years ago I was in Denmark." "That's true," Yunior agrees. "And half of me was in Africa" (85).

Issues and complications that arise from race, culture, and class often manifest in Díaz's fiction. For example, a suitable counterpart for "Flaca" is "How to Date a Browngirl, Blackgirl, Whitegirl, or Halfie" in *Drown*. While in that earlier story we get all manner of hypothetical reactions to situations that center on the girl's race, in "Flaca" there is a concrete realization of the incompatibilities that often are merely suggested in Díaz's fiction. The two characters live in different neighborhoods, even though Flaca is from Paterson, New Jersey. A critical factor in her character is that she is not from an affluent class. "You were whitetrash from outside of Paterson and it showed in your no-fashion-sense and you'd dated niggers a lot. I said you had a thing about us and you said, angry, No, I do not" (82). Despite being from a similar class as Yunior, she still resides in a different cultural sphere. When she arrives at Yunior's apartment at the opening of the story, he reminds her several times that she should roll up the windows to her car. "Someone's going to steal it," Yunior cautions.

The story moves quickly from the current interaction between Yunior and Flaca to previous moments they have shared. Often Yunior punctuates his narration with the phrase, "I remember." These are memories that are poignant for Yunior. Unlike the memories of Magda that smack of regret for his destructive behavior, or of the highly volatile Alma where, again, Yunior cheats on her, here we have no indication of cheating. Yunior and Flaca don't seem to realize they are in something like a relationship. His behavior is passive; if she wants to come over he's not going to refuse. His recollection announces his naïveté at the time: "It wasn't supposed to get serious between us. I can't see us getting married or nothing and you nodded your head and said you understood. Then we fucked so that we could pretend that nothing hurtful had just happened" (81). Always in the stories Yunior narrates readers are privy to an older, wiser Yunior, one who has ostensibly learned something of his hardships and heartaches. Along with the tone of regret that suffuses the narration, one has the feeling that Yunior wishes desperately to go back to that younger version of himself and talk a bit of sense into him.

His boys appear as peripheral reminders of the kind of man Yunior ought to be. Collectively they exert a kind of peer pressure on Yunior, and that pressure reinforces his behavior modeled after what Magda calls the typical Dominican man. Yunior is quite aware of how his boys see him: "I'd say yes and while I waited for you I'd tell the boys it's just sex, you know, nothing at all. And you'd come, with a change of clothes and a pan so you could make us breakfast, maybe cookies you baked for your class. The boys would find you in the kitchen the next morning, in one of my shirts and at first they didn't complain, because they guessed you would just go away. And by the time they started saying something, it was late, wasn't it?" (81). Ideally, why would Yunior care about what his boys thought about Flaca? His constant mention of how his boys interpret the way Yunior acts in a relationship is devastating. For someone who has seen Dominican men do whatever they want whenever they want, it is ironic that Yunior is tortured by the disparity that results when there is no synergy between what his heart leads him to do and what the social codes of Dominican masculinity dictate. Yunior's boys serve him as a skewed compass: "I remember: the boys keeping an eye on me. They figured two years ain't no small thing, even though the entire time I never claimed you. But what was nuts was that I felt fine. I felt like summer had taken me over. I told the boys this was the best decision I'd ever made. You can't be fucking with whitegirls all your life. In some groups that was more than a given; in our group it was not" (82). One has to wonder: what would Yunior do without his boys? In this instance, the implication is that he may have done more to commit to Flaca. Her whiteness disrupts their relationship precisely because Yunior sees Flaca as his boys see her, as his family, who would say she was too skinny, sees her. Yunior spends so much time focused on how other Dominican Americans view Flaca that he pays little heed to the fact that he might be in love and happy with her.

Indeed, Flaca does appear to have many of the qualities that make her a suitable partner for Yunior, her race notwithstanding. They are both highly literate: "You're the only person I've ever met who can stand a bookstore as long as I can. A smarty-pants, the kind you don't find every day" (83). They met while taking a Joyce class, and they will ultimately share the same vocation: teaching. After a time, when Flaca is gone, Yunior notices her absence. He stays up late, unable to sleep: "I figured this staying up meant something. Maybe it was *loss* or *love* or some other word that we say when it's too fucking late but the boys weren't into melodrama. They heard that shit and said no" (86). Even when Yunior is on the cusp of heeding his emotions, his boys intervene. They grant no quarter for heartfelt sincerity, and Yunior lacks the wherewithal to follow his instinct rather than masculine expectations.

It is no surprise when Flaca leaves Yunior. She doesn't leave his life completely, as she remains a powerful memory. But again we return to the second-person narration that drives the story. The story's conclusion illuminates why Díaz uses this narrative device with such aplomb: "You whispered my full name and we fell asleep in each other's arms and I remember how the next morning you were gone, completely gone, and nothing in my bed or the house could have proven otherwise" (87). Because Flaca has left long before the narration occurs, she remains a ghostly narratee, outside of earshot of a love letter directed at her. But as is typical of Díaz's use of second-person narration, it reveals a depth and complexity of Yunior's character. Without it, Yunior appears superficial and egotistical. Certainly that is how many women, Flaca included, may have seen him at the time of their respective relationships. Here the second-person narration serves as an attempted intervention that cannot remake the past. How much of the narration comprises what Yunior wishes he had said to Flaca at the time, as a way of articulating what he was feeling? Thus, the narrative never reaches its intended audience, or perhaps it was never intended for Flaca at all. Like so many of Yunior's stories, "Flaca" is meant for Yunior and no other.

In "The Sun, the Moon, the Stars," "Alma," and "Flaca," Díaz highlights Yunior's shortcomings as a boyfriend, as well as his realization that he has made many blunders in his relationships. While it is easy to situate Yunior's lack of compunction and respect in his relationships in the contexts of Dominican male machismo and the very tangible pressures Yunior's father, brother, and boys exert on him, Díaz does not give his primary narrator such an easy way out. That Yunior has taken the time to weave these stories that place him as the clear transgressor complicates the reader's engagement with him. It is difficult to feel sorry for Yunior; he is a man who freely admits his shortcomings. However, when reading *all* of the stories that concern Yunior, one cannot shake the feeling that much of his shortcomings originated from the social and cultural pressures that have impinged upon Yunior for his entire life. In some ways Yunior is a character not unlike Richard Wright's Bigger Thomas—a black man who lashes out violently against white America but does so only as a result of the systematic oppression he has known his entire life. For Yunior, the pressure he feels resides in his capacity to be a man—a Dominican American man—in a society that is at the very least more aware of its misogyny now than at any other time in its history. All of the Yunior stories have led to the final story in the collection, both literally and as it pertains to Yunior's complexity as a character.

"THE CHEATER'S GUIDE TO LOVE"

The culminating story of *This Is How You Lose Her* is a tour de force, in no small measure, because of the emotional arc Yunior traces for himself. Again, Yunior serves as a narrator critical of himself. Again, Yunior narrates to himself in the second person, covering a span of five crucial years in his life. Again, Díaz uses the "how-to" technique from "How to Date a Browngirl, Blackgirl, Whitegirl, or Halfie," this time posing as a guide to love from a cheater's perspective. There is an overt machismo imbued in the story's title. This story is not just about dating. It's about *cheating*. And who better to write the guidebook than Yunior de Las Casas? Here Díaz has a little sport with his character as well as his audience. It can now be said that Yunior wrote the (guide)book on cheating.

When Yunior narrates: "Your girl catches you cheating," he's talking about himself *to* himself. Narratologically speaking, he serves as both narrator and narratee. In the span of five years, readers catch echoes of similar situations in earlier stories. When the fiancée finds out he's been cheating with no less than fifty women over the course of six years, Yunior desperately takes her on a trip to the Dominican Republic, Mexico, and even New Zealand. There are striking similarities here with a similar ploy that occurs in "The Sun, the Moon, the Stars." In an attempt to win her back, "You try every trick in the book," including, "You blame your father. You blame your mother. You blame the patriarchy. You blame Santo Domingo" (176). As I've argued above, many of these environmental, contextual pressures *can* be said to bear some of the responsibility for Yunior's actions. And, like in "Alma," Yunior attributes his weakness to his writing: "You claim that you were sick, you claim that you were weak—It was the book! It was the pressure!—and every hour like clockwork you say that you're so so sorry" (176). But in spite of all of his attempts to make things right, to repair the damage done by his own hand, he fails.

After his first year, Yunior turns the blame on her and goes back to his typical sexual behavior, and his boys support this return to the status quo. But he's now relocated to Boston, and his emotions continue to get the better of him. The specter of racism appears once more, only this time directed at Yunior while he is in Boston. It angers and frustrates him: "You take it all very personally. I hope someone drops a fucking *bomb* on this city, you rant. This is why no people of color live here. Why all my black and Latino students leave as soon as they can" (178–79). Yunior is in Boston precisely because he cheated on his fiancée, and so finding himself the target of racist hate circles back to the fact that he is a cheater. But this is a cheater's guide to love, so Yunior continues to map the topography of cheating by giving real consequences—real because they happened to him—thinly veiled as hypothetical scenarios. But because the events narrated are so detailed, it is no surprise that Yunior has had to deal precisely with what he's describing.

In earlier stories, as I've suggested, there lurks a powerful emotionality that confronts Yunior. Often he doesn't know how to handle it, or he deflects it with wry humor. But in "The Cheater's Guide to Love" the emotionality become overwhelming and debilitating: "During finals a depression rolls over you, so profound you doubt there is a name for it. It feels like you're being slowly pincered apart, atom by atom" (179). Just how devastating does Yunior feel his depression to be? "Like someone flew a plane into your soul. Like someone flew two planes into your soul" (180). Thoughts of suicide cross his mind though he claims he "ain't the killing-yourself type" (180). In only the first year since the breakup with his fiancée, Yunior's stalwart emotional infrastructure begins to fracture and threatens to collapse.

Year two is marginally better. Yunior's depression is made manifest in the more than forty pounds he gains. He resolves to turn things for the better. His friend through this tumultuous time is Elvis, and as would be typical of Yunior's boys, he recommends that Yunior find another girl. Yunior describes the process of healing in a manner that sounds like he is overcoming addiction—only in his case, as he mentions early in the story, he is a sex addict. When he begins to "cut it out with all the old sucias" (182), it's as if he were an alcoholic ridding himself of all of the stashed liquor bottles in all the old hiding places. He meets Noemi, a Dominican, who is a good-hearted woman with a young son named Justin. But when Noemi refuses to have sex with Yunior, even after four weeks, he reverts to his sucio self: "Within an hour she has deleted you from Facebook. You send one exploratory text to her but it is never answered" (185). Noemi's rejection sends him back into a depression, and it reveals just how fragile Yunior is despite his macho exterior.

Writing, that which has proven to be a positive outlet for Yunior for most of his life, finally comes to the fore as a means of self-help. During this time of failed but therapeutic writing, Yunior finds a new addiction: running. It is an apt metaphor; Yunior has been figuratively running from something throughout the many stories in which he appears. Yunior's running transforms his body, if not his psyche. But yet again his body fails him, this time in the form of plantar fasciitis. It is yet another important aspect of his life that has been wrenched from him. New obsessions follow, such as yoga—traditionally viewed as a physical activity that seeks to unite mind and body. His body fails him once more: "It's all going swell, going marvelous, and then in the middle of a sun salutation you feel a shift in your lower back and *pau*—it's like a sudden power failure. You lose all strength, have to lie down" (190). With a ruptured disk, Yunior is invalided for a couple of weeks.

Although Yunior receives setback after setback, he is always looking for another way to release his pent up physicality—whether by running, yoga, walking, biking, or calisthenics. The occasional sex partners are unsatisfying and are rarely around for long. All of this is, in part, an indication of Yunior's age. He is far from the young boy we encountered in "Ysrael," following his older brother to see the boy with no face. He is not the young boy going out into the New Jersey winter to play with the white children. The young, inexperienced boy who found himself in Miss Lora's apartment wondering about the end of the world has gone by the wayside. Yunior's world did not end up in the apocalypse he feared as a youth. Now he battles with his crumbling body and disintegrating love life. The strange feeling in his arms and legs causes Yunior to ruminate on his mortality. But before he can ruminate too much, Yunior is confronted with the possibility that he is the father of a child. One of the few women with whom he has a minor relationship after the breakup with his fiancée is a younger woman he simply calls "the Harvard law student." Suddenly, despite all of his efforts to the contrary, Yunior has become his father. He receives the news badly: "You don't know what to say or how to act, so you bring her upstairs. You lug up the suitcases despite your back, despite your foot, despite your flickering arms. She says nothing, just hugs her pillow to her Howard sweater. She is a Southern girl with supremely straight posture and when she sits down you feel as if she's preparing to interview you. After serving her tea you ask: Are you keeping it?

"Of course I'm keeping *it*" (195).

Here is the moment where Yunior is poised to do things differently than his mostly absentee father. In the midst of Yunior's doubt—as to whether or not the child is his, or what he ought to do—Elvis admits that he has recently impregnated a girl on a recent trip to the Dominican Republic. Yunior is aghast at the entire situation, and his journal reveals his frustration, written in italics: "*Only a bitch of color comes to Harvard to get pregnant. White women don't do that. Asian women don't do that. Only fucking black and Latina women. Why go to all the trouble to get into Harvard just to get knocked up? You could have stayed on the block and done that shit*" (198). Year four is the year in which Yunior continues to tackle falsehoods, only now the emphasis is fatherhood and patrimony. Though he has doubts that he is the child's father, he allows the law student to stay with him in his apartment, despite the fact that she kicks him out of his bed and forces him, bad back and all, to sleep on the couch.

When Yunior's friend Elvis admits to having a son back in the Dominican Republic, Yunior is taken aback. Throughout this section, the false paternity of the law student's child—it turns out the baby isn't Yunior's—as well as Elvis's discovery that his son is not his, call attention to the father/son relationship. The result is that, during the fourth year after Yunior's breakup, the shadow of his father casts a shadow over his life. Yunior is tormented by having to care for a woman carrying a child that he is not even certain is his. For Yunior, hell is not some dubious afterlife torture chamber: "In the shower, the only place in the apartment you can be alone, you whisper to yourself: *Hell, Netley. We're in Hell*" (199). In the meantime, because Yunior does not yet know if he is indeed the child's father, he begins to prepare for the responsibility of parenthood, wondering, for instance, what kind of child he might have: "Whether it will be a boy or a girl, smart or withdrawn. Like you or like her" (199).

Throughout Yunior's adulthood, in taking on the numerous sexual partners that have come and gone, he has never been in the position to consider what might happen *after* he has had sex. He has never experienced the psychological and physical strain of preparing to have a child. By the time he receives a text stating that the law student has gone into labor, he is at the border of belief. That he might indeed be the father has finally become concrete in his mind. When the attendant at the hospital desk asks him if he is the father, he returns: "I am," though he adds the adverb "diffidently" (200). His public profession of his fatherhood is a detail that is hard to ignore. Just as he is prepared to enter the delivery room, to be there to watch his child being born, the law student yells, "*I don't want him in here. I don't want him in here. He's not the father*" (201). It is a crushing rejection.

"You didn't think anything could hurt so bad," Yunior confesses (201). If "The Cheater's Guide to Love" is about the possibility of a new beginning, as the story's end suggests, then Yunior must be utterly demolished for such a reset to occur. His body continues to fail him throughout the story, his best efforts for naught, and now his "lying cheater's heart" (213) must also be demolished if the possibility of redemption is to be made real. Yunior's experience is heartbreaking, soul-crushing, as when the law student's girlfriend arrives at his apartment to collect her things: "You're not going to go psycho on me, are you?" she asks Yunior (201). Her remark offends and hurts Yunior: "Why would you say that? I've never hurt a woman in my life. Then you realize how you sound—like a dude who hurts women all the time." His realization is powerful because he recognizes not only that he sounds like someone who hurts women, he *has* hurt women all his adult life. What else do cheaters do if not destroy the ones they cheat and betray? Yunior post-engagement life is like a death by a thousand cuts, each one laying him a bit barer than the last.

His false experience as a father, which to him felt real at least for a few months, consistently brings his thoughts back to his ex-fiancée. Embarrassingly, he calls her, leaving the message: "We should have had a kid" (202). He doesn't even know why he said that, though it is clear his recent experience with the law student's pregnancy has made him at least consider the possibility that he needed the responsibility of having a child.

This conclusion is another false solution, as Elvis's experience with his son reveals. The entire sequence with Elvis flying to the Dominican Republic to visit his son and the boy's mother, the revelation that Elvis is not the boy's father, and Elvis's angry rejection of the boy all illuminate Yunior's own potential as a father as well as fatherhood as some sort of solution to his ills. Elvis's story cannot help but remind Yunior of his father. As Yunior observes Elvis with his children, Díaz emphasizes what Yunior sees, always with the intent of making the literal viewing an opportunity for reflection of Yunior's life vis-à-vis Ramón. When Elvis prepares to leave for the Dominican Republic, Yunior watches as Elvis says his goodbyes: "You are at his house when he bids his wife and mother-in-law and daughter goodbye. His daughter doesn't seem to understand what's happening but when the door shuts she lets out a wail that coils about you like constantine wire. Elvis stays cool as fuck. This used to be me, you're thinking. Me me me" (202).

The scene plays out like a memory in Yunior's mind. He was the crying child unable to understand where his father was going and why he would be gone for so long. While the child cannot articulate the reasons for her distress, Yunior certainly can. In an instant he is cast back to childhood, and now recognizes the pain he felt at the hands of his father's callous and reckless behavior. Yunior, who did not know where his father would go, now can make the trip alongside Elvis. It is as if he is walking stride for stride with his father all those years ago.

When Yunior sees the squalor in which Elvis's son lives, it is an opportunity for readers to see just how far Yunior has traveled—from the place of his and his father's birth as well as along his development as a person. He suddenly becomes protective of Elvis Jr.—another junior like himself—and he connects to the boy in ways he shouldn't. Yunior describes him: "He is a piercingly cute carajito. He has all these mosquito bites on his legs and an old scab on his head no one can explain to you. You are suddenly overcome with the urge to cover him with your arms, with your whole body" (205). Yunior sees the potential in the boy; "MIT-bound," he thinks. But more than that, he cannot help but see himself in the boy. In a rare moment of self-lessness, Yunior feels a great empathy for Elvis Jr. That's why, even after he realizes that Elvis Jr. is not Elvis Sr.'s son, he implores the father to continue to send money and help whenever he can. After all, the indiscretions and deplorable behavior by the parents are not the child's fault. And Yunior, who has narrated so many stories of his childhood, understands that fact all too well. But in another way, Elvis Jr. could have been Yunior's son, and he cannot help but see the boy through the eyes of a parent: "The boy holds on to you tightly. There is no significance in this, you tell yourself. It's a Moro-type reflex, nothing more" (207). Yunior's invocation of the Moro reflex, tested when babies are born, is suggestive of the paternal attitude he takes toward Elvis Jr.

This section of the story, year four, culminates as Yunior and Elvis take Elvis Jr. to the clinic to undergo a paternity test. Elvis's refusal to admit the truth—that Elvis Jr. is not his son—relates to both his conception of fatherhood and his trauma resulting from his time as a soldier in Iraq: "But I always wanted a boy. . . . My whole life that's all I wanted. When I got in that shit in Iraq I kept thinking, Please God let me live just long enough to have a son, please, and then you can kill me dead right after. And look, He gave him to me, didn't He? He gave him to me" (207). Elvis's confession is a rare moment of emotional expression by any of the Dominican men in any of Díaz's stories, let alone by one of Yunior's boys. But the tenderness Elvis expresses cannot be read as the desire to have a healthy relationship with his son. The fact that he prays to God for a son, rather than a child, is yet another expression of male virility and power. It is fitting, then, that his misguided though answered prayer is quickly and efficiently undone by a simple blood test.

Four weeks later, as year five opens, Elvis confirms what Yunior intuited during their trip to the Dominican Republic. Elvis's acrimony over having been lied to disturbs Yunior: "Fuck, [Elvis] says bitterly, fuck fuck fuck. And then he cuts off all contact with the kid and the mother. Changes his cell phone number and e-mail account. I told that bitch not to call me again. There is some shit that can't be forgiven" (208). Unlike Yunior, who did not have the time to bond with a child that might not have been his own, Elvis has thought of Elvis Jr. as his son for over three years. The disparity between Yunior's and Elvis's reaction to the knowledge says something of Yunior's growth as a person—and, more importantly, his understanding of the complexities of manhood—during the years after his breakup. While Elvis can only rage against Elvis Jr.'s mother, Yunior's thoughts are solely for the boy: "Of course you feel terrible. You think about the way the boy looked at you. Let me have her number at least, you say. You figure you can throw her a little cash every month but he won't have it. Fuck that lying bitch" (208).

This moment is extraordinary, and it is further evidence of Yunior's growth. Elvis feels the lying as a betrayal, angered that he was taken so easily. As one of Elvis's boys, Yunior should have been there for him. Instead, Yunior is so moved by the boy back in the Dominican Republic that he wants to send some of *his* money to help support the boy and his mother. Through Elvis's situation, Yunior shows his capacity for empathy and forgiveness. He cannot understand how Elvis can be so unyielding: "With him it's like nothing happened. You wish you could be as phlegmatic" (208).

As Yunior becomes more emotionally sensitive, now with the capacity to understand the consequences of decisions made in relationships, his body's continued deterioration continues unabated. Upon the diagnosis of spinal stenosis—a narrowing of the spine that leads to significant numbness in various parts of his body, Yunior grows more sensitive to his feelings. Thus, as his body becomes numb and unfeeling, his ability to engage and recognize his world emotionally is as heightened as it has ever been.

Through it all, Yunior cannot come to terms with the loss of his fiancée. He asks, desperately, how long it will take to move beyond the pain of his loss. His answers are so varied that they are of little use. It is not until he confronts what he sardonically calls "The Doomsday Book"—a collection "of all the e-mails and fotos from the cheating days, the ones the ex found and compiled and mailed to you a month after she ended it. *Dear Yunior, for your next book.* Probably the last time she wrote your name" (212). In reading the evidence of his cheating, he is finally convinced that he deserved what he got. He reflects, "You are surprised at what a fucking chickenshit coward you are. It kills you to admit it but it's true. You are astounded by the depths of your mendacity. When you finish the Book a second time you say the truth: You did the right thing, negra. You did the right thing" (212).

It is important that Yunior not consider The Doomsday Book until his fifth year after his breakup. Everything that has happened to him in the interim was absolutely required in order for him to make an actual evaluation of the transgressive nature of his cheater's behavior during his relationship. When he comes to the realization that "The half-life of love is forever" (213), readers understand that Yunior's entire life—his childhood, his preadolescence, his brother, his father, his cheating—has brought him to the brink of this moment. For Yunior, the possibility of surviving the consequences of his actions rests in the curative powers of writing: "The next day you look at the new pages. For once you don't want to burn them or give up on writing forever" (213). For five years, Yunior has been surviving. Through it all, he can begin once again. As he now understands, "sometimes a start is all we ever get" (213).

This Is How You Lose Her is an appropriate culmination for Yunior as a character. Throughout the many stories in which he appears, his actions and attitudes make it easy for a reader to at once be smitten and repulsed. His witty repartee and achingly beautiful insight reveal the charm and personality that makes him so attractive to the many women who enter into his life. Conversely, his willingness to cheat on women who love him and the often callous actions he takes may cause readers a certain amount of discomfort. The culminating story of the collection strips away all that has come before, and one gets the sense that, despite its appearance as the final story, this may have been the story that truly initiates Yunior as a writer. It indicates, perhaps, that all of these stories ostensibly written by Yunior serve as a sort of ongoing therapy where his imagination and memory can interact with the craft of writing. How much more poignant to read a story such as "Ysrael" or "The Pura Principle" with the knowledge that he is writing at a time *after* "The Cheater's Guide to Love." Such an understanding increases the distance between the time of the narrated events and the time of the narration. While we can't confirm Yunior wrote all of these stories post–"Cheater's Guide," it cannot be discounted so easily. But if we allow for this possibility, it is easy to argue that so many of Díaz's stories must be read as a contiguous unit of narrative—an overarching storyworld in which a character such as Yunior can develop and grow beyond a position of self-centeredness. Yunior can only understand the world—and himself—through writing. Whether it's television, film, comics, novels,

poetry, a Doomsday Book, or a Cheater's Guide to Love, Yunior—
and by extension, Díaz—understand the transformative and healing
power of writing. Ultimately, his discovery of self can occur only
through the authorship of his stories.

CHAPTER 4

Uncollected Fiction and Nonfiction

"MONSTRO"

"Monstro" is a short story that originally appeared on June 4, 2012, in the *New Yorker*'s science fiction issue. As a part of Díaz's novel in progress, the story continues the author's penchant for postapocalyptic and speculative fiction and also his preference for the Dominican male narrator with women on his mind. While there are hints and overt strains of science fiction and apocalypse that pervade his fiction, and he truly engages with speculative fiction in *The Brief Wondrous Life of Oscar Wao*, "Monstro" marks the first occasion for Díaz to pursue this particular genre of storytelling outright, with the central concern of the narrative a deadly outbreak of disease.

As a stand-alone story, "Monstro" leaves much untold. But as an excerpt of a larger novel, we would expect many of the gaps that are left unattended to be filled to some degree. A retrospective narrator tells the story, and initially, the narrator speaks in a style similar to Yunior's. That is to say, he uses many of the same techniques for invoking humor and poking fun at a serious situation that Yunior uses. For instance, consider the opening line: "At first, Negroes thought it *funny*. A disease that could make a Haitian blacker? It was the joke of the year. Everybody in our sector accusing everybody else of having it. You couldn't display a blemish or catch some sun on the street without the jokes starting. Someone would point to a spot on your arm and say, Diablo, haitiano, que te pasó?"[1] The narrator, unnamed throughout the story, gives the colloquial designation for the disease: "La Negrura . . . The Darkness."[2]

The story owes an enormous debt to postapocalyptic fiction, particularly those tales in which the apocalypse is brought about by an aggressively virulent disease. Whereas the 1980s heralded an apocalypse brought about by a mutually assured nuclear bombardment, the other literary device for wiping out the vast majority of humanity is a type of engineered or mutant virus. Stephen King, a prominent literary touchstone in *Oscar Wao*, authored one of the most influential novels set in a virus-triggered postapocalypse, *The Stand*. There have been others. John Wyndham's 1951 novel *The Day of the Triffids*—a novel referenced by Yunior in *Oscar Wao*[3]—Max Brooks's *World War Z*, and, more recently, Peter Heller's *The Dog Stars* all explore how a tiny band of humanity's remaining population can go from a position of merely surviving to actually living, with the comforts and culture humanity had before the onset of apocalypse.

However, Díaz's story is a crucial addition to the Latino/a literary tradition. Postapocalyptic narratives often do away with people of color—or at least their larger concerns in a white hegemonic society—because the postapocalyptic narrative functions as a kind of reset button where survivors either band together or strive against one another for reasons other than culture or the melanin level of their skin. King does create an African American principal character, a Moses figure, a figure of goodness, in Abagail Freemantle, known as "Mother Abagail" in *The Stand*. Octavia Butler's *Parable of the Sower* and Samuel R. Delany's *Dhalgren* are major novels of the genre written by authors of color. In Heller's novel, a highly touted book from 2012, there are seemingly no people of color in the postapocalypse. Protagonists and antagonists alike are hewn from a monochromatic majority. Consider, too, Alfonso Cuarón's film *Children of Men* in which the one character of color becomes a sort of

New Eve for humanity. Yet among all critically significant works of Latino/a literature there appears no contribution to the postapocalyptic genre, though an argument could be made that *all* of Latino/a literature is postapocalyptic if one reads the conquest of Aztlán and other Mesoamerican native peoples as apocalypse.

Still, Díaz's story and the resulting novel brings much-needed diversity to this tradition of fiction. The narrator, who has survived the outbreak, is Dominican. A majority of the narrative recounts events that occur on the island of Hispaniola, and recasts the historical divisiveness between Dominicans and Haitians in a new context. The narrator is our guide during this chaotic outbreak of disease, echoing the technique Max Brooks used to great effect in *World War Z*, subtitled *An Oral History of the Zombie War*. The narrator in "Monstro" weaves his oral history of the apocalypse, yet he also reveals highly personal aspects of his life. In fact, he places the blame for his suffering on himself:

> These days everybody wants to know what you were doing when
> the world came to an end. Fools make up all sorts of vainglorious
> self-serving plep—but me, I tell the truth.
>
>   I was chasing a girl.
>
>   I was one of the idiots who didn't heed any of the initial reports,
> who got caught way out there. What can I tell you? My head just
> wasn't into any mysterious disease—not with my mom sick and all.
> Not with Mysty.
>
>   Motherfuckers used to say culo would be the end of us. Well, for
> me it really was.[4]

"Monstro" progresses along two inexorably converging tracks. Slowly but steadily, the disease—La Negrura—spreads across Haiti and the Dominican Republic. At the same time, the then nineteen-year-old narrator, an aspiring writer attending Brown University, falls in love with a girl named Mysty, "a ridiculously beautiful mina."[5] Mysty has a close relationship with Alex, the narrator's friend from Brown, who is handsome, an artist, and a photographer. The narrator is smitten by Mysty:

> In those days she was my Wonder Woman, my Queen of Jaragua, but the truth is I don't remember her as well as I used to. Don't have any pictures of her—they were all lost in the Fall when the memory stacks blew, when la Capital was scoured. One thing a Negro wasn't going to forget, though, one thing that you didn't need fotos for, was how beautiful she was. Tall and copper-colored, with a Stradivarius curve to her back. An ex-volleyball player, studying international law at UNIBE, with a cascade of black hair you could have woven thirty days of nights from.[6]

In retrospect, Mysty's beauty endures beyond the terrors of the apocalypse. This juxtaposition of beauty and horror, echoing Oscar's final written words and the closing words of *The Brief Wondrous Life of Oscar Wao*—words that themselves echo Kurtz's closing utterance in Conrad's *Heart of Darkness*—yields a tension and lingering regret in the narration of "Monstro."

Similarly, there is dramatic tension that arises as a consequence of the distance in time from the events that are narrated and the time in which the narration occurs. Because the narrator is relating something that is part memoir, part oral history, we can assume several things that are never confirmed in the story but may be in the resulting novel. First, the narrator is a survivor of the apocalypse. We know that, of course. After all, he is narrating with the benefit of hindsight—although, because this story is part of a larger work that is not yet complete, there remains the possibility that the narrator is dead, something like what we find in Mexican author Juan Rulfo's *Pedro Paramo*, Alfredo Vea Jr.'s *La Maravilla*, or Marlon James's *A Brief History of Seven Killings*. Second, the narrator uses particular words that exist only within the storyworld of "Monstro"—words like the verb "glypt," which is a type of electronic message, as well as slightly different spellings for common words such as "viktim" and "Krimea."

These literary devices, used by authors such as Anthony Burgess and Sesshu Foster, serve as signposts for the reader, subtle cues that suggest a changed world that is similar to yet very different from our own. Third, the story ends with Alex charging off to the Haitian-Dominican border to photograph all hell breaking loose, with the narrator and Mysty going with him. Because of the story's lack of closure, let alone ending, a full analysis of it is akin to analyzing one chapter of *The Brief Wondrous Life of Oscar Wao.* Therefore, I will not attempt a comprehensive critical analysis of "Monstro." Instead, I will draw out the salient aspects that reveal why this story and (assuming Díaz will complete it) the novel are important interventions in Latino/a speculative fiction.

Why should Díaz's foray into speculative fiction be such a significant development in American literature, generally speaking? To begin with, science fiction, though necessarily based in a human conception of the universe (i.e., the narrative must be somewhat recognizable to a contemporaneous human reader even if it takes place in the far future or in a distant part of the universe), has the freedom to portray a reality that is vastly different from our own. Sesshu Foster can create an interdimensional being that visits realities where the Aztecs were not conquered by the Spanish, but, rather, the Spanish were run out of the Americas. Octavia Butler's clear-eyed critique of American slavery is made so powerful because she uses the literary device of time travel within her novel *Kindred.* And while there have been a few notable instances of Latino/a narratives that embrace the speculative genres—one thinks readily of Isabela Rios's novel *Victuum* and Alex Rivera's independent film *Sleep Dealer*—Díaz brings visibility (thanks to his Pulitzer Prize for Fiction, as well as his MacArthur genius grant) to Latinos in speculative fiction.

That "Monstro" takes place primarily outside of the United States, on the island of Hispaniola, is a fact that instantly changes the dynamic of the narrative, especially for an American author whose writings are categorized, generally speaking, as American literature.

Like his contemporary, American author Daniel Alarcón, who has set most of his fiction in an undisclosed area of South America while writing for an English-speaking American audience, Díaz has a trans-American sensibility to his fiction. Not only does he, like Alarcón, spend a great deal of his time in Latin America, so too does his fiction continually negotiate US and Dominican spaces, alternately and with ease.

In fact, the narrator makes a conscious decision to remain in the Dominican Republic and refuses to come to the United States when he has the opportunity:

> Let me not forget this—this is the best part. Three days before it happened, my mother flew to New Hialeah with my aunt for a specialty treatment. Just for a few days, she explained. And the really best part? *I could have gone with her!* She invited me, said, Plenty of culo plastic in Florida. Can you imagine it? I could have ducked the entire fucking thing.
>
> I could have been safe.[7]

Going against the diasporic trend of fleeing to the United States, the narrator decides to remain in the Dominican Republic, as he mentions early in the story, for a girl. At least within the confines of "Monstro" the narrator provides eyewitness accounts of the apocalypse as it unfolds outside of the US border.

The story is filled with the fodder of science fiction: electromagnetic pulses, the infected humans that "sing," a six-hundred-mile "dead zone" where electronic devices no longer operate, and "forty-foot-tall cannibal motherfuckers running loose on the Island."[8] As with all good speculative fiction, "Monstro" forces readers to see the humanity of its characters by stripping away the chaff.

NONFICTION

Díaz has published several pieces of autobiographical nonfiction as well as articles on subjects ranging from food to coming to New York

City to his fascination with the apocalypse. These essays illuminate the author's biography, and discerning readers will see echoes of these pieces in Díaz's fiction. But it is important to resist the impulse to read his fiction as autobiography—a challenge because Díaz and his narrator, Yunior, have much in common. The texts analyzed in the following are a selection of Díaz's nonfiction.

"My First Year in New York; 1995"
PUBLISHED IN THE *NEW YORK TIMES*, SEPTEMBER 17, 2000

This very short piece (approximately five hundred words) was part of a group of similar pieces by notable figures concerning their first sustained experience with New York. Díaz begins by acknowledging his father as the first of his family to experience life in New York, detailing the grueling work conditions he faced in the early 1970s. Ironically, his father left New York City for New Jersey before Díaz ever reached the United States. Though he would finally come to NYC in 1995, the city at night seemed to him "like science fiction" when he was a child. Despite its brevity, this article crystallizes the near fantastical qualities a city like New York has for an émigré. Díaz likens it to Oz, "The City of Everything," "like an incubator for the stars," rendering his disappointment in ultimately growing up in New Jersey all the more poignant. Just as in other essays, there is the sense here that Díaz's relationship with his father is key to understanding him as a writer. In this piece, the two are paralleled: his father with the "'usual' Caribbean immigrant experience"; Díaz with the "usual Caribbean college-graduate experience."

"Homecoming, with Turtle"
PUBLISHED IN THE *NEW YORKER*, JUNE 14, 2004

As the title indicates, Díaz recounts his return trip to the Dominican Republic, after being in the United States for twenty years. Not only is his homecoming a literal one, in many respects it is a metaphorical one. It is an opportunity to come back to his land of birth and remember many aspects of his culture, as well as to hone his Spanish. Díaz notes that he left for New Jersey at the age of six and made his return trip as a twenty-six-year-old. And, like Yunior in "The Sun, the Moon, the Stars," Díaz returned with his girlfriend in the hopes that he could repair some of the damage he caused by cheating on her. In fact, this essay sounds so much like "The Sun, the Moon, the Stars" that it is easy to think it a work of fiction. Díaz relates how the "ex-sucia" sent his girlfriend a letter detailing the entire affair (a similar event plays a large part in "The Cheater's Guide to Love"), and the trip seems to be a weak but sincere opportunity to put the relationship back together. At its heart, the essay lays bare Díaz's insecurities with his Dominican bona fides and his level of comfort when speaking Spanish. Unlike the confident Yunior, who is embarrassed to stay at the tourist resorts in "The Sun, the Moon, the Stars," Díaz invariably erred in the knowledge of the island. Locals could not believe he was Dominican and insisted on calling him an American, much to his chagrin. His tussle with a mounted turtle that decorated his hotel wall punctuates his sense of displacement; he attacked the turtle after his girlfriend mistakenly thought it was an intruder in the darkened room. After many return trips after his breakup, Díaz feels more comfortable with his nation of birth and his mother tongue while the locals continue to see him as a "gringo."

"It's at a crossroads like this that you really learn something about yourself," Díaz muses, speaking of the terror of believing an intruder has entered your bedroom. It is indeed a fight or flight moment, and Díaz invokes his father's militaristic admonitions to "always attack," no matter the situation. This ability to persevere through anything life throws at you, be it the breakup with a girlfriend, feeling like a stranger in your native land, or grappling with your cultural-linguistic heritage, provides momentum to the entire essay. Díaz also positions himself as a work-in-progress, someone who, unlike Yunior, has to work on his Spanish and his Dominican identity. In fact, the uncertain relationship with the Dominican Republic echoes Oscar de León more than it does Yunior. Yet because there are so many similarities between this essay and some of Díaz's fiction, it has the unfortunate effect of stoking the idea that his fiction is mostly auto-biographical, or that it ought to be read as such. The essay gives few indications that it is indeed an essay rather than fiction, resulting in a piece of writing that blurs the line between fiction and nonfiction.

"*Summer Love, Overheated*"
PUBLISHED IN *GQ: GENTLEMEN'S QUARTERLY*, AUGUST 2008

Here Díaz chronicles a failed relationship with a woman named Amelia, "from Amsterdam, black Dominican mother, white Dutch father." In a brief paragraph, Díaz describes Amelia in such a way that there is little wonder as to why he was in love with her:

> She was about the most exotic Dominican woman I'd ever met (that's the kind of shit that matters to you when you're in your twenties), and the classiest. She spoke Spanish and could dance bachata, but she'd grown up in the farthest spiral reaches of the diaspora, in Delft, Vermeer's old stomping ground. Was smart, too; could speak four other languages, had traveled all over the world, and could tell a story like you and I can tell a lie. She was finishing her thesis on Domin-ican women's identity, but what she really wanted to do was write children's stories. She wanted to be the next Roald Dahl. Every now and then, especially when she was excited, she would forget articles and misconjugate her verbs. She'd pick up her camera and say, I want to make picture. I found it incredibly endearing.

Though there is plenty of the expected physicality of relation-ships that tends to appear in Díaz's writing, here he shines a light on his own emotional and psychological shortcomings, a rhetorical move that is equally tender and brave. He would place the relationship's failing completely in himself, even if Amelia craved male attention a bit more than he would have liked. At any rate, he was too jealous, too insecure, too depressed: "The shit should have been perfect, perfect, except for the fact that I was basically nuts. I was depressed, experienced alarming mood swings, and suffered from what a psychologist called baseline irritability (which meant that I could go from zero to violent in 2.2 seconds)."

His admission is revealing; his depression even affected his writing, his livelihood. As he made one last bid for reconciliation with Amelia, Díaz recounts a traumatic episode involving the drowning of a dog. A Dutch man, playing fetch with his two dogs by the lake, fails to notice the smaller dog go under water and not resurface: "I was the only one who noticed the poor fuck go under. Your dog, I told the guy. Fate would have it that he was the lone motherfucker in Holland who didn't speak English. What is it? my girlfriend asked me. His dog is drowning, I screamed, and that's when she cried to him in Dutch and the dude, giving out an anguished cry, jumped right into the lake." With his depression deepening, Díaz would go on to blame the demise of the relationship on the dog. But with his final line, "Of course I did," he signals his awareness of the irrationality of this sort of thinking. Because he is looking back on his relationship with Amelia, Díaz appears as being wiser for the experience. But he also displays the power of looking at his past self with a fairly critical eye.

"The Taste of Home"
PUBLISHED IN GOURMET, AUGUST 2006

When you have a "locura" for Japanese food, a fourteen-hour-long trip to Japan appears quite logical. Díaz unfurls his passion for Japanese food in this essay that highlights his penchant for flying to Japan, in part to indulge his taste for its cuisine. The essay also serves as a retrospective for how he gained such an ardor for non-Dominican food when many Dominicans don't: "Many Dominicans from my class background, at least from my experience, tend to be unwilling to eat anything *other* than Dominican food," he writes. The source of his sense of adventure when it comes to food is his father, an "angry and brutal" man who had grown an appetite for the variety of non-Dominican foods he found in the United States. His father was less brutal when he was cooking: "To be honest these were like some of the only times he was at peace in the house. He never yelled or struck any of us when he was cooking. We could sit in the living room and not worry about when the other shoe would fall or hit us upside our heads. Our very own Chinese Food Armistice. One of the last memories I have of my old man was of him making one of his Chinese meals and then voila, like that he was gone and I never really saw him again."

Díaz makes an essay about his taste in food about the problematic relationship with his father during his childhood. Díaz tacitly suggests that one of the lasting influences his father had on him was this free-ranging palate. The vast array of foods quickly became associated with his father, so that necessarily, when Díaz's father left him at a young age, non-Dominican foods such as Japanese and Chinese cuisine seemingly served as a stand-in for his loss. Once his father left for good, Díaz spent his money on indulging his diverse taste in food. If his mother made a meal he was unhappy with, he would leave to eat elsewhere: "But at least once a week, like clockwork, like ceremony, I had to have a meal at this Szechwan restaurant up the street that I loved. Not a fancy place but the ingredients were fresh and the cook had a bit of swing. I never ate with anybody and nobody really knew I did it. Just me by myself. It wasn't until much later that I figured out what I was doing. Back then I just thought I was eating something I really really liked."

Throughout the essay, Díaz moves in and out of a myriad of linguistic codes and highly specialized allusions, as he often does in his fiction. The difference here is that his essay calls for a reader well versed in Japanese culture and cuisine. There are well-known references to "kaiju kits," *Sailor Moon*, and St. Mark's Street in New York City, and perhaps less well-known invocations of such words as *gaijin* (foreigner), *gyozo* (similar to wonton), and *loh-fan* (foreigner). Because there are many seeds of historical fact in Díaz's fiction, this essay further illuminates how he shapes the father figure, and Yunior's father especially, in his stories.

"The Dreamer"
APPEARED IN *MORE*, MAY 2011

Díaz has also written of his mother, demonstrating that her courage and resolve to get an education directly influenced his determination to be a writer. In "The Dreamer" he reminds readers that not everyone has such easy access to education as children do in the United States. As she was born into a farming family in the Dominican Republic, Díaz's mother would have remained a farm worker in perpetuity, "a mule," as he states, if not for her passion for education, rooted in her experiences nursing injured farmworkers. He also credits a decree passed by Trujillo that all Dominican children would get an education and go to school. The only power that could override Díaz's maternal grandmother was an injunction by Trujillo himself. Díaz's mother was willing to drink from a festering pool of water that made her sick to avoid going off to harvest coffee beans. While her mother was gone, she reported to the school.

The essay underscores Díaz's appreciation for education, but it also hints at where he gets his dogged resolve. Whereas his father was hardworking but unwilling to see a commitment through, Díaz's mother readily met any challenge presented to her. In other essays where Díaz discusses his ability to persevere through hopelessness that he might fail in his writing, we clearly see that, though his father may have literally beaten lessons of perseverance in his sons, Díaz was bestowed this inherited trait from his mother. And though one must always be careful when juxtaposing historical fact and narrative fiction, one can at least see a source of inspiration for the undaunted Belicia Cabral in *The Brief Wondrous Life of Oscar Wao* in Díaz's mother.

"*Dispatches from the Apocalypse: What Disasters Reveal*"
PUBLISHED IN *BOSTON REVIEW*, MAY 1, 2011

In this eight-sectioned essay, Díaz addresses the massive 7.0 magnitude earthquake that reduced so much of Haiti to rubble on January 12, 2010. "It was," he says with sobering directness, "for all intents and purposes an apocalypse." Using James Barger's conception of three types of apocalypses—the end of everything, something that seems like the end of everything, the end that illuminates—Díaz launches into an exploration of the last of these, or "how the Haiti earthquake was also an apocalypse of the third kind, a revelation." For Díaz, an apocalyptic event is an opportunity to glimpse insight into our future, what he calls "ruin-reading." That is to say, there is a possible positive that comes from such a devastatingly negative event.

Díaz adopts a solemn tone throughout the essay (after all, nearly a quarter of a million people died in the earthquake, to say nothing of the more than one million people seriously impacted by the disaster). There is little of the irreverence, black humor, or irony that one typically finds in Díaz's writing, though he does invoke Harry Potter and the Eye of Sauron. As a result, the essay necessarily reveals a different aspect of his prose. He punctuates his claims with alarming statistics, such as "In Haiti life expectancy hovers at around 60 years as compared to, say, 80 years in Canada." Because he invokes the biblical book of Revelation and likens an apocalypse to the process of revelation, many of the essay's sections end with the quasi-biblical statement, "And this too the earthquake revealed." Amid such penetrating logic that suggests the hopelessness of the postapocalypse, Díaz continually brings readers back to powerful moments in which we might be hopeful, such as the example of a Dominican woman who left her infants at home in order to nurse Haitian babies, newly orphaned. With an unabashed eye, Díaz critiques the conditions that exacerbate these apocalypses, such as the Fukushima nuclear plant disaster that occurred while he was revising his essay. But the more

he peers into the apocalypse, the more he finds hope: "One day somewhere in the world something terrible will happen and for once we
will heed the ruins. We will begin collectively to take responsibility
for the world we're creating. Call me foolishly utopian, but I sincerely
believe this will happen. I do. I just wonder how many millions of
people will perish before it does." In addition to being an exploration of human calamity, the essay provides an understanding of Díaz's
conception of the nature of apocalypse, a notion that looms large in
his fiction, and in particular, *The Brief Wondrous Life of Oscar Wao*. The
essay informs his notion of "ruin-reading," something that "requires
nuance, practice, and no small amount of heart. I cannot, however,
endorse it enough. Given the state of our world—in which the very
forces that place us in harm's way often take advantage of the confusion brought by apocalyptic events to extend their power and in
the process increase our vulnerability—becoming a ruin-reader might
not be so bad a thing. It could in fact save your life." In this light, what
is Yunior if not a ruin-reader?

"The Dominican Republic's War on Haitian Workers"
(with Edwidge Danticat)
APPEARED IN THE *NEW YORK TIMES*, NOVEMBER 20, 1999

Junot Díaz and Edwidge Danticat make a potent dyad of American writers who were born in the Caribbean. Of the same generation, Díaz and Danticat are as committed to political activism as
they are to their writing, as evidenced in this *New York Times* piece
from November 20, 1999. In it, Danticat and Díaz discuss a border
conflict that is rooted in difficult manual labor and exploitative labor
practices—a conflict not unlike the one the United States has with
Mexico and the nations that make up Central America. The two writers highlight the Dominican Republic's perennial practice of tolerat-
ing Haitian laborers to work the Dominican sugar cane fields, now
complicated by the advent of more mechanical farming practices that
have reduced the need for such a large human workforce. As a result,

Díaz and Danticat argue, the Dominican government has exacerbated this already tense situation by deporting individuals of Haitian descent who have lived in the Dominican Republic, often for many years. The Dominican law at the time, like that of the United States, granted citizenship to individuals born on native soil. The two nations similarly refuse citizenship for the foreign-born parents of such children. Both writers make a point to draw explicit connections between the mass deportations of Haitians and the brutal regime of Dominican dictator Raphael Trujillo and the massacre of Haitians in 1937.

The article is striking for its resonance with the US predicament of the undocumented and of immigration reform. In the fifteen years since the publication of this article, Díaz has publicly denounced many anti-Haitian political developments in the Dominican Republic, only to have his "Dominicanness" refuted by politicos in the Dominican Republic. At the same time, the political climate in the United States surrounding undocumented immigrants, and especially the ever-increasing wave of refugee children who have crossed into the United States, pushes the situation of national borders, undocumented labor, and deportations to the breaking point. Díaz and Danticat form a powerful alliance, and their writings show the union of discourse and politics. This essay also serves as a reminder that, while fiction has an inherent trait of retraining the attention of its readers to political matters, it is actual activism, such as the kind found in this article, that pushes the potential of fiction into the arena of the political. Such political pronouncements by artists carry potential risks in terms of their careers, but both Díaz and Danticat are writers who do not mince words.

"Storyteller-in-Chief"
APPEARED IN THE *NEW YORKER ONLINE*, JANUARY 10, 2010

Díaz furthers this idea of the power of narrative as having an almost inherent political quality. When faced with even a mediocre story, Díaz seems to say, the man of facts and reason cannot contend.

Here Díaz levels a major critique of President Barack Obama, not for his policies or ideas but rather for his inability to weave a story toward which the nation might gravitate. According to Díaz, Obama's detractors gain such hearty support because they have the semblance of a story. In contrast, Díaz has a major expectation that President Obama fails to meet: "It has always seemed to me that one of a President's primary responsibilities is to be a storyteller."

Perhaps it is no surprise that such a respected storyteller in his own right would criticize a president who cannot tell those stories that the nation craves. In truth, Díaz views the Obama administration as lacking the kind of power to drive through the sorts of policies progressives would like to see enacted. But he would also know how storytellers, and particularly those superb storytellers who practice politics, can have overriding sway over the people. The power of narrative is evident in Díaz's fiction. For instance, Yunior knows full well the sort of world-creating power he wields in his writing. And dictators such as Trujillo and Balaguer were able to run roughshod because their narratives had the might of a brutal regime to prop them up. In this essay, Díaz seems to forecast the extreme political right as handily winning the storytelling game. He suggests that despite the impressive storytelling prowess Obama had evinced before he became president, his administration utterly lacks the motivating, inspiring force an engaging narrative provides.

"How I Became a Writer"
APPEARED IN *O, THE OPRAH MAGAZINE*, OCTOBER 2009

Several of Díaz's essays illuminate his development as a writer. The dominant thread in these essays is that nothing comes easily to Díaz when he is crafting his fiction. Whereas some writers seemingly write with ease and grace, Díaz characterizes his process as agonizing and anxiety producing, particularly after writing *Drown*, which, he suggests, was relatively easy. In "How I Became a Writer," Díaz discusses the period after the success of *Drown* and his progress on his second novel. There were several false starts, each of them running out of steam after around seventy-five pages. Indeed, the impetus for the essay seems to be the oft-asked question Díaz receives concerning the ten years that span the publication of *Drown* and *The Brief Wondrous Life of Oscar Wao*. "It wasn't that I couldn't write," he confesses. "I wrote every day. I actually worked really hard at writing. At my desk by 7 A.M., would work a full eight and more. Scribbled at the dinner table, in bed, on the toilet, on the No. 6 train, at Shea Stadium. I did everything I could. But none of it worked." A vicious cycle ensued. The more he was unable to produce acceptable pages, the more he began to doubt his abilities.

Rather than give up, Díaz persisted. The essay is remarkable in its laying bare the difficulties of writing. Though it took him a decade to finish his second book, the quality of the final product, if accolades and awards are any valid measures, is hard to ignore. But the essay reveals most of all how Díaz came to view himself as a writer. As he puts it, "In my view a writer is a writer because even when there is no hope, even when nothing you do shows any sign of promise, you keep writing anyway." Here Díaz opens the curtain to reveal that, unlike the imagined scenario of a perfect writing situation that will allow one to pen the next masterpiece, most likely a writer will be confronted with less-than-ideal conditions that are not conducive to the creative process. It is at this moment, in his view, that the real writer is forged.

"Loving Ray Bradbury"
APPEARED IN THE *NEW YORKER ONLINE*, JUNE 6, 2012

"The truth is, for me, and for a whole generation of readers, I'm sure, Bradbury is never far from mind," Díaz writes in his short paean to the legendary Ray Bradbury, who had just died at the age of ninety-one at the time of the essay's publication. Díaz recalls the great impact Bradbury had on him, and with effective poignancy recalls the moment he read Bradbury's story "All Summer in a Day" as a child still struggling with English. In the story, a little Earth girl named Margot is a new arrival to the rain-soaked planet Venus. On Venus, the sun shines for only one hour once every seven years. The Venusian children bully Margot and lock her in a closet right at the critical moment when the sun shines on Venus, consequently forcing her to miss the warmth and radiance of the sun she enjoyed so much back on Earth. Of "All Summer in a Day," Díaz says: "I read that short tale, and when I came to those ruthless final lines I was shattered by them. In the back of the Madison Park library I read that story and cried my little eyes out. I had never been moved like that by any piece of art. I had never known what I'd been experiencing as an immigrant, never had language for it until I read that story. In a few short pages, Bradbury gave me back to myself." So influential was this story on Díaz that an allusion to it appears in *Oscar Wao*: "Sucks a lot to be left out of adolescence, sort of like getting locked in the closet on Venus when the sun appears for the first time in 100 years."[9]

As in his fiction, and particularly in *Oscar Wao*, Díaz demonstrates how important science fiction and fantasy can be, especially to immigrants and children of color. Like Tolkien, Stephen King, and others, Bradbury provided new ways of seeing old problems in his creative endeavors, of capturing these insights in the form of narratives. Such powerful stories have helped shape Díaz as an individual and as a writer, and in turn, have enabled him to create influential stories.

"Introduction"
FROM *DISMANTLE: AN ANTHOLOGY OF WRITING FROM THE VONA/VOICES WRITING WORKSHOP* (2014)

It is fitting that the final piece discussed in this book is Díaz's introduction to *Dismantle: An Anthology of Writing from the VONA/Voices Writing Workshop*. This essay, the most recent of Díaz's publications discussed in this book, also appeared in a condensed version as "MFA vs. POC" in the *New Yorker Online* on April 30, 2014. It takes readers back to a time before the accolades and prizes, when Díaz was an MFA student at Cornell University. If the number of responses that appeared on blogs and websites to the excerpted piece is any indication, there were many people who took umbrage with Díaz's characterization of the MFA system as "too white." Many deemed his takedown of the system from which he seemingly benefited as hypocritical and ungrateful. The essay, in part, also reveals his personal struggle in a prestigious writing program—a struggle to fit in, to write freely, to thrive in a community. Like Sandra Cisneros's similar lambasting of the Iowa Writers' Workshop, Díaz mostly argues that his literary success comes *despite* his time in Cornell's MFA program, not because of it. It is an assertion that was destined to offend some people, but that has rarely been one of Díaz's concerns when writing.

The essay charts Díaz's entry into a writing career. He notes his near-painful naïveté regarding what to expect in an MFA program; he had imagined the experience would nurture him in a "supportive environment." But the reality was vastly different from his expectations: "In fact by the start of my second year I was like: *get me the fuck out of here.*"[10] For Díaz, the problem was the whiteness of the program, a problem he calls "standard." Rather than being an opportunity to explore creative writing from a multitude of engagement points, Díaz notes, the monocular advancement of a myopic approach to writing was inherent in the MFA system. There was little acknowledgment of race and the issues that concern people of color (POC), let alone an approach for crafting this sort of literary writing. "In my workshop," Díaz writes, "the default subject position of reading and writing—of *Literature* with a capital Gothic L—was white, straight and male."[11]

In hindsight, knowing what we know of Díaz's approach to writing, one can readily recognize how his aesthetic and thematic desires for fiction would not be nurtured in an environment such as the Cornell MFA program he attended. (Cornell did hire writer Helena María Viramontes, but only after Díaz was nearly done with his program. In fact, he notes his efforts to advocate for her hire.) If we consider creative writing before the rise of the MFA system from a

Latino/a perspective, the difficulty in convincing publishers of the possibility that readers might enjoy and be moved by a novel written by a Latino/a about Latinos is apparent. If the MFA system was intended to provide a methodical approach to the craft of writing, a restrictive view of what counts as "*Literature* with a capital Gothic L" would further burden Latino/a writers by either invalidating the stories they wanted to tell or compelling them to write a literature that can best be described as whitened. Instead of motivating the multifaceted capacity of storytelling, the MFA system creates a normative conception of narrative that does not necessarily reflect the diverse readership that beckons.

Many of the critiques Díaz and his two fellow writers of color in the Cornell MFA program faced still haunt the sorts of reader comments one hears in classrooms and reads in reviews on sites such as Goodreads and Amazon; e.g., "Why is there even Spanish in this story?" If fellow writers in a graduate program—writers who are ostensibly superb readers—cannot see the value in the diverse life experiences that motivate certain types of storytelling, and thereby invalidate those diverse life experiences themselves, what chance do such writers as Díaz have with the average reader who reifies so-called great American writing as that of, say, Jonathan Franzen? Díaz implies a change from within over time is the only means of addressing the problem. He recommends that writers of color apply to and stay in MFA programs. Why? It is the only way of providing ample opportunities for universities and workshops to hire faculty of color, just as it happened with Viramontes. In order to hire writers of color, there must *be* writers of color.

The essay also contrasts what happened to Díaz, who ultimately finished his program and went on to write the fiction that motivates most of this book, with what happened to a fellow MFA student he calls "Athena," a writer who, for Díaz, serves as an exemplar of the MFA system gone wrong. Athena, tired of the whiteness of the program, made the difficult decision to leave Cornell. Díaz writes,

"Of course I tried to get her to stay. Shit, I would have gotten on my knees if I thought it would have changed her mind. Selfish shit really; I just didn't want to be alone in that workshop but she didn't change her mind."[12] Athena is but one example of a writer of color the MFA system neglected, rather than nurtured and encouraged to create the kind of writing that moved her. One wonders how many writers of color have met with a similar fate.

Díaz's essay also provides a rationale for the Voices of Our Nation Arts Foundation (VONA) workshop, of which he is a cofounder. The VONA/Voices workshop serves as a small but significant move to correct the whiteness of the MFA system. Because of his "stubbornness" and sheer ability to keep moving forward with a career in writing, Díaz's talent and skills had the opportunity to be noticed. Athena, on the other hand, at least according to Díaz, was a writer of such great potential that the absence of her voice in American literature seems to trouble Díaz. In this respect, one cannot help but invoke the notion of the *página en blanco* that functions as a supportive pillar in so much of Díaz's writing. One cannot help but wonder at the thousands upon thousands of blank pages that could have, and arguably should have, been filled with the writings of so many writers of color. For Díaz, the MFA system, with its potential to give voice to those writers who want to inscribe their own blank pages, ultimately exacerbates the silence. It is a blistering appraisal of MFA programs and should cause the system to reconsider further how it does or does not recognize, validate, or otherwise engage with the life experiences of people of color.

When Junot Díaz published his first short story, "Ysrael," in 1995 in the literary journal *Story*, few might have guessed that he would achieve such critical acclaim on the backs of two short story collections and one novel. His works have become required readings in college courses, and his quips about language and writing regularly appear on social media and are used in internet memes. He has appeared on *The Colbert Report* to discuss his work and his efforts with Freedom University. In short, he has already attained an influential role in discussions of Latinos, literature, and popular culture. There are several critical factors that make Díaz such an impactful writer.

First, Díaz has a clear and obvious passion for literary and cultural storytelling practices. As he often displays in his writing, he has as much facility with the great works of literature as he does the minutiae of superhero comics. In interviews, he is eager to share works of literature that have impressed him to a high degree, and those works range the gamut of form and genre. He speaks of these works the way some people talk about the times close friends have comforted them during rough times. Indeed, often it appears he is much more at ease discussing works of literature other than his own. His exuberance for reading and writing, for not heeding the divisions between highbrow and lowbrow culture, make Díaz an impassioned advocate for literacy, storytelling, and activism—particularly in the Latino/a community.

As a result of the passion he has for literature, popular culture, and freedom of expression, he has no problem being irreverent, both in his writing and in live speaking engagements. The word *fuck* and its variants punctuate Díaz's speech like flashes of lightning. Despite his forays into the fantastical, his ear for the spoken word gives his writing a firm foundation in realism. Like Piri Thomas and Oscar "Zeta" Acosta before him, Díaz shapes his storyworlds with the language of real people. In that sense, his narrators are as steeped in realism as any other encountered in American fiction. Thus, his fiction simultaneously breaks new ground while adhering to well-established tradition in American letters. In many ways, he brings several traditions together.

To be sure, as I have argued throughout this book, Díaz's greatest achievement to date is his narrator Yunior de Las Casas. In contemporary American literature, perhaps only Philip Roth's Nathan Zuckerman stands above Yunior. Díaz's narrator is one of the reasons his works stand out so prominently. Consider, for example, how his stories that feature a third-person narrator do not seem to convey the same sort of kinetic volatility inherent in Yunior's narration. Because Yunior is a narrator who is a writer, his narration always has a whiff of being a carefully constructed piece of writing. And, because Yunior is also an author, he is not simply a memorable character narrator. As his stories accumulate, he grows more complex in a reader's mind, even when Yunior is telling someone else's story. As he goes through his life and gets older, with his body beginning to fail him, he is not unlike Zuckerman, who searches for vitality and meaning in the lives of others in the group of novels that have come to be known as Philip Roth's American trilogy (*American Pastoral*, *I Married a Communist*, and *The Human Stain*). Yunior has several more books to go before he is a narrator on par with Zuckerman, but he is certainly on his way.

Finally, the idea of the *página en blanco* is in many ways an apt metaphor for Díaz's writings. The notion of a blank book—an uninscribed volume lying dormant somewhere—indicates the problem of invisibility and blankness with which Latino/a authors have struggled. When we think about the unwritten book, we wonder *why* the book remains unwritten. Is it that the writer has nothing to say? Is it that no one would read the book anyway? Is it that the publisher does not want to take the risk of publishing the writer's story? Whence comes the silence?

In American literature, there are silences that haunt like ghosts. For too long the idea of an American literature did not include the voices of Latinos who had compelling and worthwhile stories to tell. Until Latino/a authors can freely adopt and employ any technique of narrative form and select the thematic content of their choosing, American literature will fall short of reflecting an ever-growing segment of the nation's Latinos. Similarly, the silences that permeate Díaz's fiction hearken to the thwarted flourishing of a Latino/a literary tradition. On the other hand, Díaz gives us a glimpse of where Latino/a literature may be headed in years to come. His bold decisions that lead to the creation of complex Latino/a characters and storyworlds, of intricate interplay of Latinidad and masculinity, and of transnational historiography and intertextual literacies compel readers to rethink Latinos, and consequently, how they conceive of America in the twenty-first century.

NOTES

INTRODUCTION

1. Ramón Saldívar, "Historical Fantasy, Speculative Realism, and Postrace Aesthetics in Contemporary American Fiction," *American Literary History* 23, no. 3 (2011): 574.

2. Diogenes Cespedes and Silvio Torres-Saillant, "Fiction Is the Poor Man's Cinema: An Interview with Junot Díaz," *Callaloo* 23, no. 3 (2000): 894.

3. Cespedes and Torres-Saillant, "Fiction Is the Poor Man's Cinema," 901.

4. Ilan Stavans, ed., *The Norton Anthology of Latino Literature* (New York: Norton, 2011), 2351.

5. Albert Jordy Raboteau, "Conversation with Junot Díaz: (To the Woman in the Mountain Cabin)," *Callaloo* 31, no. 3 (2008): 920.

6. Junot Díaz, interview by Edwidge Danticat, *BOMB*, Fall 2007, 89.

7. See José David Saldívar, "Conjectures on 'Americanity' and Junot Díaz's 'Fukú Americanus' in *The Brief Wondrous Life of Oscar Wao*," *Global South* 5, no. 1 (2011): 120–36.

8. Junot Díaz, "Introduction," *Dismantle*, ed. Marissa Johnson-Valenzuela (Philadelphia: Thread Makes Blanket Press, 2014): 1.

9. Díaz, "Introduction," *Dismantle*, 3.

10. Sandra Cisneros, *Leonard Lopate Show*, 93.9 WNYC, April 23, 2009.

11. A quotation from Cisneros serves as the epigraph to *This Is How You Lose Her*.

12. Ilan Stavans, *Spanglish: The Making of a New American Language* (New York: Rayo, 2003), 6.

13. Cespedes and Torres-Saillant, "Fiction Is the Poor Man's Cinema," 904.

14. Rune Grauland, "Generous Exclusion: Register and Readership in Junot Díaz's *The Brief Wondrous Life of Oscar Wao*," *MELUS* 39, no. 3 (2014): 34.

15. William Anthony Nericcio, *Tex[t] Mex: Seductive Hallucinations of the "Mexican" in America* (Austin: University of Texas Press, 2007).

16. Stavans, *Norton Anthology of Latino Literature*, 2352.

CHAPTER 1. *DROWN*

1. John Riofrio compellingly argues that *Drown* is a novel. While I don't think the book has the unity and cohesiveness of a novel, I do support the idea that the stories cohere to a singular effect when read together. To my thinking, *Drown* is closer to a short-story cycle. See Riofrio, "Situating Latin American Masculinity: Immigration, Empathy, and Emasculation in Junot Díaz's *Drown*," *ATENA* 28, no. 1 (2008): 23–36.

2. Cespedes and Torres-Saillant, "Fiction Is the Poor Man's Cinema," 892.

3. Riofrio, "Situating Latin American Masculinity," 26.

4. Junot Díaz, *Drown* (New York: Riverhead, 1996), 5. Cited parenthetically by page number hereafter within this chapter.

5. Riofrio, "Situating Latin American Masculinity," 28.

6. Natalie J. Friedman, "Adultery and the Immigrant Narrative," *MELUS* 34, no. 3 (2009): 83.

7. "Playing the dozens is an African American verbal street game of escalating insults. In different communities, it is also called woofing, sounding, joning, screaming, cutting, capping, and chopping, among other things. There is a slight shift in the rules from place to place." Edward Hirsch, *A Poet's Glossary* (New York: Houghton Mifflin Harcourt, 2014), 177.

8. Daniel Bautista, "In and Out of the Mainstream: Dominican-American Identity in Junot Díaz's 'How to Date a Browngirl, Blackgirl, Whitegirl, or Halfie,'" *Romance Notes* 49, no. 1 (2009): 83.

9. Marisel Moreno, "Debunking Myths, Destabilizing Identities: A Reading of Junot Díaz's 'How to Date a Browngirl, Blackgirl, Whitegirl, or Halfie,'" *Afro-Hispanic Review* 26, no. 2 (2007): 106.

10. For more about "positions of privilege," see Peter J. Rabinowitz, *Before Reading: Narrative Conventions and the Politics of Interpretation* (Columbus: Ohio State University Press, 1987).

11. Dorothy Stringer, "Passing and the State in Junot Díaz's 'Drown,'" *MELUS* 38, no. 2 (2013): 121.

CHAPTER 2. *THE BRIEF WONDROUS LIFE OF OSCAR WAO*

1. Saldívar, "Historical Fantasy," 585.

2. Monica Hanna, "'Reassembling the Fragments': Battling Historiographies, Caribbean Discourse, and Nerd Genres in Junot Díaz's *The Brief Wondrous Life of Oscar Wao*," *Callaloo* 33, no. 2 (2010): 500, 504.

3. Daniel Bautista, "Comic Book Realism: Form and Genre in Junot Díaz's *The Brief Wondrous Life of Oscar Wao*," *Journal of the Fantastic in the Arts*, no. 1 (2010): 42.

4. Anne Garland Mahler, "The Writer as Superhero: Fighting the Colonial Curse in Junot Díaz's *The Brief Wondrous Life of Oscar Wao*," *Journal of Latin American Cultural Studies* 19, no. 2 (2010): 120.

5. Junot Díaz, *The Brief Wondrous Life of Oscar Wao* (New York: Riverhead, 2007), 1. Cited parenthetically by page number hereafter within this chapter.

6. Saldívar, "Conjectures on 'Americanity,'" 133.

7. See *Images that Injure: Pictorial Stereotypes in the Media*, 2nd ed., ed. Paul Martin Lester and Susan Dente Ross (Westport, CT: Greenwood, 2003), 236–40.

8. Stavans, *Norton Anthology of Latino Literature*, 2352.

9. Jennifer Harford Vargas, "Dictating a Zafa: The Power of Narrative Form in Junot Díaz's *The Brief Wondrous Life of Oscar Wao*," *MELUS* 39, no. 3 (2014): 8–9.

10. Elena Machado-Sáez, "Dictating Desire, Dictating Diaspora: Junot Díaz's *The Brief Wondrous Life of Oscar Wao* as Foundational Romance," *Contemporary Literature* 52, no. 3 (2011): 523–24.

11. Katherine Weese, "Tú no Eres Nada de Dominicano': Unnatural Narration and De-Naturalizing Gender Constructs in Junot Díaz's *The Brief Wondrous Life of Oscar Wao*," *Journal of Men's Studies* 22, no. 2 (2014): 102.

12. Literally, "blank page." The term tends to represent an omission or erasure in the historical record. In Díaz's novel, there are several such instances of gaps in the narrative, as well as lost manuscripts and letters that purport to have significant answers—such as the manuscript Oscar promises to send Yunior, which never arrives. Díaz's novel itself can thus serve as an attempt to reinscribe, however imperfectly, an omission in the historical record.

13. Antonio Olliz Boyd, *The Latin American Identity and the African Diaspora: Ethnogenesis in Context* (Amherst, NY: Cambria Press, 2010), 25.

14. Juanita Heredia, "The Dominican Diaspora Strikes Back: Cultural Archive and Race in Junot Díaz's *The Brief Wondrous Life of Oscar Wao*," in *Hispanic Caribbean Literature of Migration: Narratives of Displacement*, ed. Vanessa Pérez Rosario (New York: Palgrave Macmillan, 2010), 209–10.

15. George Reid Andrews, *Afro-Latin America* (New York: Oxford University Press, 2004), 140.

16. This act of genocide has been the impetus for several works of fiction, including Julia Alvarez's *In the Time of the Butterflies*, Edwidge Danticat's *The Farming of Bones*, and Mario Vargas Llosa's *The Feast of the Goat*.

17. Silvio Torres-Saillant, "The Tribulations of Blackness: Stages in Dominican Racial Identity," *Callaloo* 23, no. 3 (2000): 1107.

18. Specifically, Railton locates his investigation of what he terms "meta-realism" on four such narrators: Carraway, Zuckerman, Willa Cather's Jim Burden, and Yunior. However, Railton unproblematically casts Yunior as a "novelist-narrator," when Yunior has clearly written a book that, if he were an actual person, we would call nonfiction. It is a significant detail that makes Yunior's document stand out in American fiction. Within US Latino literature, the narrative style in *The Brief Wondrous Life of Oscar Wao* has a progenitor in Oscar "Zeta" Acosta's two novels, *The Autobiography of a Brown Buffalo* and *The Revolt of the Cockroach People*. Both Díaz's and Acosta's texts feature unfettered narrators who set about the task of documenting historical events. One crucial difference, however, is subject: Acosta testifies to the "Brown Buffalo" (i.e., himself), while Díaz (through Yunior) testifies to Oscar and his family. See Ben Railton, "Novelist-Narrators of the American Dream: The (Meta-)Realistic Chronicles of Cather, Fitzgerald, Roth, and Díaz," *American Literary Realism* 43, no. 2 (2011): 133–53.

19. Díaz, *Drown*, 5.

20. Díaz, *Drown*, 30.

21. Díaz, *Drown*, 143.

22. Melissa D. Birkhofer, "Voicing a Lost History through Photographs in Hispaniola's Diasporic Literature: Junot Díaz's 'Aguantando' and Edwidge Danticat's 'The Book of the Dead,'" *Latin Americanist* 52, no. 1 (2008): 45.

23. Torres-Saillant, "Tribulations of Blackness," 1097.

24. Torres-Saillant, "Tribulations of Blackness," 1097.

25. Yunior allows Lola to narrate parts of her story in this section titled "Wildwood," and she is the only character afforded such a privileged position. For all of Yunior's seeming machismo, he has no hesitation in exalting strong Afro-Dominican women in his book.

26. "Junot Díaz: The New Fiction Hero," interview by Rachel Chambers, *Art Culture: Contemporary Art, Innovation and Design*, February 27, 2009.

27. Junot Díaz, interview by Carrie Meathrell and Osmany Rodriguez, *LAist*, April 10, 2008.

28. Junot Díaz, "What Obama Means to Me," with Maya Angelou, Kara Walker, Gloria Steinem, Scott Turow, Wanda Sykes, Nadine Gordimer, and Anna Devere Smith, *Newsweek*, January 27, 2009, 123–24.

29. Raboteau, "Conversation," 921.

30. Tim Lanzendörfer, "The Marvelous History of the Dominican Republic in Junot Díaz's *The Brief Wondrous Life of Oscar Wao*," *MELUS* 38, no. 2 (2013): 129.

31. Charles Hatfield, *Hand of Fire: The Comics Art of Jack Kirby* (Jackson: University Press of Mississippi, 2012), 132.

32. Hatfield, *Hand of Fire*, 132.

33. Hatfield, *Hand of Fire*, 133.

34. Hatfield, *Hand of Fire*, 3.

35. Hatfield, *Hand of Fire*, 3.

36. Hatfield, *Hand of Fire*, 12.

37. Hatfield, *Hand of Fire*, 16.

38. Junot Díaz, interview by *The Progressive*, March 8, 2008.

39. "But the 'consolation' of fairy-tales has another aspect than the imaginative satisfaction of ancient desires. Far more important is the Consolation of the Happy Ending. Almost I would venture to assert that all complete fairy-stories must have it. At least I would say that Tragedy is the true form of Drama, its highest function; but the opposite is true of Fairystory. Since we do not appear to possess a word that expresses this opposite—I will call it Eucatastrophe. The eucatastrophic tale is the true form of fairy-tale, and its highest function." See J. R. R. Tolkien, "On Fairy Stories," *Tolkien on Fairy Stories*, ed. Verlyn Flieger and Douglas A. Anderson (New York: HarperCollins, 2008), 22.

40. Susan Johnson, "*Harry Potter*, Eucatastrophe, and Christian Hope," *Logos* 14, no. 1 (2011): 69.

41. Tolkien, "On Fairy Stories," 68.

42. J. R. R. Tolkien, *The Lord of the Rings* (Boston: Houghton Mifflin, 1994; first published 1954–55 by Allen & Unwin), 924.

43. Tolkien, *Lord of the Rings*, 925.

44. Sindarin is one of Tolkien's invented Elvish languages.

45. Graulund, "Generous Exclusion," 37.

46. Graulund, "Generous Exclusion," 37.

CHAPTER 3. *THIS IS HOW YOU LOSE HER*

1. Junot Díaz, *This is How You Lose Her* (New York: Riverhead, 2012), 3. Cited parenthetically hereafter within this chapter.

2. Ana María Manzanas Calvo, "Junot Díaz's 'Otravida, Otravez' and *Hospitalia*: The Workings of Hostile Hospitality," *Journal of Modern Literature* 37, no. 1 (2013): 109.

CHAPTER 4. UNCOLLECTED FICTION AND NONFICTION

1. Junot Díaz, "Monstro," *New Yorker*, June 4, 2012, 107.

2. Díaz, "Monstro," 107.

3. Díaz, *Oscar Wao*, 320.

4. Díaz, "Monstro," 107.

5. Díaz, "Monstro," 110.

6. Díaz, "Monstro," 110.

7. Díaz, "Monstro," 117.

8. Díaz, "Monstro," 118.

9. Díaz, *Oscar Wao*, 23.

10. Díaz, "Introduction," *Dismantle: An Anthology of Writing from the VONA/ Voices Writing Workshop*, ed. Marissa Johnson-Valenzuela, Andrea Walls, Adriana E. Ramirez, Camille Acker, and Marco Fernando Navarro (Philadelphia: Thread Makes Blanket Press, 2014), 1–2.

11. Díaz, "Introduction," 2.

12. Díaz, "Introduction," 6.

BIBLIOGRAPHY

The following bibliography, arranged in chronological order throughout, begins with a list of Díaz's own works: his books, short stories, nonfiction essays, reviews, reprinted and anthologized writings, and critical introductions and forewords. Because they may prove useful to readers, Spanish translations of Díaz's books are also included. The bibliography then lists works about Díaz and his writings: books, chapters, articles, and interviews. I close with cited and consulted works not listed in earlier parts of the bibliography.

WORKS BY JUNOT DÍAZ

Books

Drown. New York: Riverhead Books, 1996.
The Brief Wondrous Life of Oscar Wao. New York: Riverhead Books, 2007.
This Is How You Lose Her. New York: Riverhead Books, 2012.
This Is How You Lose Her. Deluxe ed. Illustrated by Jaime Hernandez. New York: Riverhead Books, 2013.

Short Stories

"Ysrael." *Story*, Autumn 1995, 25–33.
"How to Date a Brown Girl (black girl, white, girl, or halfie)." *New Yorker*, December 25, 1995, 83–85.
"Boyfriend." *Time Out New York,* 1995.
"Drown." *New Yorker*, January 29, 1996, 78–81.
"Fiesta, 1980." *Story*, Winter 1996, 10–20.
"Edison, New Jersey." *Paris Review*, Spring 1996, 333–47.

"Invierno." *Glimmer Train* 19 (Summer 1996): 7–25.

"The Sun, the Moon, the Stars." *New Yorker*, February 2, 1998, 66–71.

"Flaca." *Story*, Autumn 1999, 145–49.

"Nilda." *New Yorker*, October 4, 1999, 92–97.

"The Brief Wondrous Life of Oscar Wao." *New Yorker*, December 25, 2000, 98–104.

"Nilda." *Callaloo* 23, no. 3 (2000): 885–91.

"Watermarks." *African Voices* 9, no. 18 (2002): 18–20.

"Wildwood." *New Yorker*, June 11, 2007, 74–87.

"Alma." *New Yorker*, December 24, 2007, 52–53.

"2007: New York City: This Is How You Lose Her." *Lapham's Quarterly* 2, no. 1 (December 15, 2009): 132–133.

"The Pura Principle." *New Yorker*, March 22, 2010, 60–67.

"Miss Lora." *New Yorker*, April 23, 2012, 62–67.

"Monstro." *New Yorker*, June 4, 2012, 106–18.

"The Cheater's Guide to Love." *New Yorker*, July 23, 2012, 60–69.

Reprints

"Ysrael." In *The Best American Short Stories, 1996*, edited by John Edgar Wideman and Katrina Kenison, 86–96. Boston: Houghton Mifflin, 1996.

"Fiesta, 1980." In *The Best American Short Stories, 1997*, edited by Annie Proulx and Katrina Kenison, 157–70. Boston: Houghton Mifflin, 1997.

"Invierno." In *The 1998 Pushcart Prize XXII: Best of the Small Presses*, edited by Bill Henderson, 467–81. Wainscott, NY: Pushcart Press, 1997.

"Ysrael." In *The Art of the Story: An International Anthology of Contemporary Short Stories*, edited by Daniel Halpern, 211–19. New York: Penguin, 1999.

"The Sun, the Moon, the Stars." In *The Best American Short Stories, 1999*, edited by Amy Tan and Katrina Kenison, 15–28. Boston: Houghton Mifflin, 1999.

"Instrucciones para citas con trigueñas, negras, blancas o mulatas." In *Se habla español: voces latinas en USA*, edited by Edmundo Paz Soldán and Alberto Fuguet, 229–36. Miami, FL: Alfaguara, 2000.

"Nilda." In *The Best American Short Stories, 2000*, edited by E. L. Doctorow and Katrina Kenison, 89–97. Boston: Houghton Mifflin, 2000.

"The Sun, the Moon, the Stars." In *The Beacon Best of 1999: Creative Writing by Women and Men of All Colors*, edited by Ntozake Shange, 97–111. Boston: Beacon Press, 2000.

"The Sun, the Moon, the Stars." In *Step into a World: A Global Anthology of the New Black Literature*, edited by Kevin Powell, 213–22. New York: Wiley, 2000.

"Edison, New Jersey." *A Whistler in the Nightworld: Short Fiction from the Latin Americas*, edited by Thomas Colchie, 377–92. New York: Plume, 2002.

"No Face." In *Herencia: The Anthology of Hispanic Literature of the United States*, edited by Nicolás Kanellos, 417–20. Oxford: Oxford University Press, 2002.

"Edison, New Jersey." In *Latino Boom: An Anthology of U.S. Latino Literature*, edited by John S. Christie and José B. Gonzalez, 196–205. New York: Pearson/Longman, 2006.

"Nilda." In *The Scribner Anthology of Contemporary Short Fiction: Fifty North American Stories since 1970*, 2nd ed., edited by Lex Williford and Michael Martone, 144–51. New York: Scribner, 2007.

"Alma." In *Sudden Fiction Latino: Short-Short Stories from the United States and Latin America*, edited by Robert Shapard, James Thomas, and Ray González, 39–42. New York: Norton, 2010.

"From *The Brief Wondrous Life of Oscar Wao:* 'GhettoNerd at the End of the World 1974–1987.'" In *The Norton Anthology of Latino Literature*, edited by Ilan Stavans, 2361–73. New York: Norton, 2011.

"Ysrael." In *The Norton Anthology of Latino Literature*, edited by Ilan Stavans, 2353–61. New York: Norton, 2011.

"Miss Lora." In *The Best American Short Stories, 2013*, edited by Elizabeth Strout and Heidi Pitlor, 58–71. Boston: Houghton Mifflin, 2013.

Books in Spanish Translation

Negocios: Cuentos. Translated by Eduardo Lago. New York: Vintage Español, 1997.

La breve y maravillosa vida de Óscar Wao. Translated by Achy Obejas. New York: Vintage Español, 2008.

Así es como la pierdes. Translated by Achy Obejas. New York: Vintage Español, 2013.

Edited Anthologies

The Beacon Best of 2001: Great Writing by Women and Men of All Colors and Cultures. Boston: Beacon Press, 2001.

Articles and Nonfiction Essays

"Se han perdido los reyes" [The three kings lose their way]. In *Las Christmas: escritores latinos recuerdan las tradiciones navideñas*, edited by Esmeralda Santiago and Joie Davidow, 13–16. New York: Vintage Books, 1998.

"The Dominican Republic's War on Haitian Workers." With Edwidge Danticat. *New York Times*, November 20, 1999, A13.

"How (in a Time of Trouble) I Discovered My Mom and Learned to Live." In *Las Mamis: Favorite Latino Authors Remember Their Mothers*, edited by Esmeralda Santiago and Joie Davidow, 157–68. New York: Knopf, 2000.

"My First Year in New York; 1995." *New York Times Magazine*, September 17, 2000, 111.

"Language, Violence, and Resistance." In *Voice-Overs: Translation and Latin American Literature*, edited by Daniel Balderston and Marcy E. Schwartz, 42–44. Albany: State University of New York Press, 2002.

"Homecoming, with Turtle." *New Yorker*, June 14, 2004, 90–95.

"The Taste of Home." *Gourmet*, August 2006, 30–35.

"Cockfighting Is Cruel and Inhumane. It's Also a Way of Life." *ESPN Magazine*, March 10, 2008, 14.

"Summer Love, Overheated." *GQ*, August 2008, 104–6.

"What Obama Means to Me." With Maya Angelou, Kara Walker, Gloria Steinem, Scott Turow, Wanda Sykes, Nadine Gordimer, and Anna Devere Smith. *Newsweek*, January 27, 2009, 122–27.

"Becoming a Writer." *O, The Oprah Magazine*, November 2009, 190–91.

"One Year: Storyteller-in Chief." *New Yorker Online*, January 10, 2010. http://www.newyorker.com/news/news-desk/one-year-storyteller-in-chief.

"Tokyo." *Newsweek*, April 4, 2011, 10.

"The Dreamer." *More*, May 2011, 121, 176.

"The Money." *New Yorker*, June 13, 2011, 76.

Foreword to *Latinos, Inc: The Marketing and Making of a People*, by Arlene M. Dávila, xvii–xx. Berkeley: University of California Press, 2012.

"Introduction: Dream of the Red King." Introduction to *A Princess of Mars*, by Edgar Rice Burroughs, ix–xlviii. New York: Library of America, 2012.

"Loving Ray Bradbury." *New Yorker Online*, June 6, 2012. http://www.newyorker.com/books/page-turner/loving-ray-bradbury.

Introduction to *Dismantle: An Anthology of Writing from the VONA/Voices Writing Workshop*, edited by Marissa Johnson-Valenzuela, Andrea Walls, Adriana E. Ramirez, Camille Acker, and Marco Fernando Navarro, 1–8. Philadelphia: Thread Makes Blanket Press, 2014.

Reviews

"Shortcomings." Review of *Shortcomings*, by Adrian Tomine. *Publishers Weekly*, September 24, 2007, 42.

"'Grand,' but No 'Godfather.'" Review of *Grand Theft Auto IV*, by Rockstar Games. *Wall Street Journal*, June 28, 2008, W3.

"The Psychotic Japanese Mastermind." Review of *Monster*, by Naoki Urasawa. *Time*, July 28, 2008, 50.

CRITICAL BOOKS, CHAPTERS, AND ARTICLES ON DÍAZ

Paravisini-Gebert, Lizabeth. "Junot Díaz's *Drown*: Revisiting 'Those Mean Streets.'" In *U.S. Latino Literature: A Critical Guide for Students and Teachers*, edited by Harold Augenbraum and Margarite Fernández Olmos, 163–74. Westport, CT: Greenwood Press, 2000.

Connor, Anne. "Desenmascarando a Ysrael: The Disfigured Face as a Symbol of Identity in Three Latino Texts." *Cincinnati Romance Review* 21 (2002): 148–62.

Cowart, David. "Closet and Mask: Junot Díaz's *Drown*." In *Trailing Clouds: Immigrant Fiction in Contemporary America*, 190–204. Ithaca, NY: Cornell University Press, 2006.

De Genova, Nicholas. "Joining the State: Sexuality and Citizenship in Junot Díaz and Chang-rae Lee." In *Racial Transformations: Latinos and Asians Remaking the United States*, 147–69. Durham, NC: Duke University Press, 2006.

Suárez, Lucía M. "Exposing Invisibility: *Drown*." In *The Tears of Hispaniola: Haitian and Dominican Diaspora Memory*, 91–118. Gainesville: University Press of Florida, 2006.

Dalleo, Raphael, and Elena Machado Sáez. *The Latino/a Canon and the Emergence of Post-Sixties Literature*. New York: Palgrave Macmillan, 2007.

Di Iorio Sandín, Lyn. "The Latino Scapegoat: Knowledge through Death in Short Stories by Joyce Carol Oates and Junot Díaz." In *Contemporary U.S. Latino/a Literary Criticism*, edited by Lyn Di Iorio Sandín and Richard Perez, 15–34. New York: Palgrave Macmillan, 2007.

Frydman, Jason. "Violence, Masculinity, and Upward Mobility in the Dominican Diaspora: Junot Díaz, the Media, and *Drown*." *Columbia Journal of American Studies* 8 (2007): 270–81.

Moreno, Marisel. "Debunking Myths, Destabilizing Identities: A Reading of Junot Díaz's 'How to Date a Browngirl, Blackgirl, Whitegirl, or Halfie.'" *Afro-Hispanic Review* 26, no. 2 (2007): 9–23.

Perez, Richard. "Racial Spills and Disfigured Faces in Piri Thomas's *Down These Mean Streets* and Junot Díaz's 'Ysrael.'" In *Contemporary U.S. Latino/a Literary Criticism*, edited by Lyn Di Iorio Sandín and Richard Perez, 93–114. New York: Palgrave Macmillan, 2007.

Birkhofer, Melissa D. "Voicing a Lost History through Photographs in Hispaniola's Diasporic Literature: Junot Díaz's 'Aguantando' and Edwidge Danticat's 'The Book of the Dead.'" *Latin Americanist* 52, no. 1 (2008): 43–53.

Riofrio, John. "Situating Latin American Masculinity: Immigration, Empathy and Emasculation in Junot Díaz's *Drown.*" *Atenea* 28, no. 1 (2008): 23–36.

Wessells, Henry. "A Short and Contentious Note about *The Brief Wondrous Life of Oscar Wao* by Junot Díaz." *New York Review of Science Fiction* 20, no. 10 (2008): 10–11.

Bautista, Daniel. "Junot Díaz and the Lucha Libre." *Sargasso: A Journal of Caribbean Language, Literature, and Culture* 2 (2008–2009): 41–55.

Miranda, Katherine. "Junot Díaz, Diaspora, and Redemption: Creating Progressive Imaginaries." *Sargasso: A Journal of Caribbean Language, Literature, and Culture* 2 (2008–2009): 23–39.

Bautista, Daniel. "In and Out of the Mainstream: Dominican-American Identity in Junot Díaz's 'How to Date a Browngirl, Blackgirl, Whitegirl, or Halfie.'" *Romance Notes* 49, no. 1 (2009): 81–90.

Caminero-Santangelo, Marta, ed. "Trujillo, Trauma, Testimony: Mario Vargas Llosa, Julia Alvarez, Edwidge Danticat, Junot Díaz and Other Writers on Hispaniola." Special issue, *Antípodas: Journal of Hispanic and Galician Studies* 20 (2009).

Cox, Sandra. "The Trujillato and Testimonial Fiction: Collective Memory, Cultural Trauma and National Identity in Edwidge Danticat's *The Farming of Bones* and Junot Díaz's *The Brief Wondrous Life of Oscar Wao.*" *Antípodas: Journal of Hispanic and Galician Studies* 20 (2009): 107–26.

Flores-Rodríguez, Daynalí. "Addressing the Fukú in Us: Junot Díaz and the New Novel of Dictatorship." *Antípodas: Journal of Hispanic and Galician Studies* 20 (2009): 91–106.

Friedman, Natalie J. "Adultery and the Immigrant Narrative." *MELUS* 34, no. 3 (2009): 71–91.

López-Calvo, Ignacio. "A Postmodern Plátano's Trujillo: Junot Díaz's *The Brief Wondrous Life of Oscar Wao*, More Macondo than McOndo." *Antípodas: Journal of Hispanic and Galician Studies* 20 (2009): 75–90.

Balkan, Stacey. "'City of Clowns': The City as a Performative Space in the Prose of Daniel Alarcón, Junot Díaz, and Roberto Bolaño." In *Wretched Refuge: Immigrants and Itinerants in the Postmodern*, edited by Jessica Datema and Diane Krumrey, 89–107. Newcastle upon Tyne, England: Cambridge Scholars, 2010.

Bautista, Daniel. "Comic Book Realism: Form and Genre in Junot Diaz's *The Brief Wondrous Life of Oscar Wao.*" *Journal of the Fantastic in the Arts* 1 (2010): 41–53.

Hanna, Monica. "'Reassembling the Fragments': Battling Historiographies, Caribbean Discourse, and Nerd Genres in Junot Díaz's *The Brief Wondrous Life of Oscar Wao*." *Callaloo* 33, no. 2 (2010): 498–520.

Heredia, Juanita. "The Dominican Diaspora Strikes Back: Cultural Archive and Race in Junot Díaz's *The Brief Wondrous Life of Oscar Wao*." In *Hispanic Caribbean Literature of Migration: Narratives of Displacement*, edited by Vanessa Pérez Rosario, 207–21. New York: Palgrave Macmillan, 2010.

Ibarrola-Armendariz, Aitor. "Dominican-American Auto-Ethnographies: Considering the Boundaries of Self-Representation in Julia Alvarez and Junot Díaz." *Revista Alicantina de Estudios Ingleses* 23 (2010): 213–29.

Irizarry, Ylce. "Making It Home: A New Ethics of Immigration in Dominican Literature." In *Hispanic Caribbean Literature of Migration: Narratives of Displacement*, edited by Vanessa Pérez Rosario, 89–103. New York: Palgrave Macmillan, 2010.

Irr, Caren. "Media and Migration: Danticat, Díaz, Eugenides, and Scibona." In *Wretched Refuge: Immigrants and Itinerants in the Postmodern*, edited by Jessica Datema and Diane Krumrey, 9–26. Newcastle upon Tyne, England: Cambridge Scholars, 2010.

Jay, Paul. *Global Matters: The Transnational Turn in Literary Studies.* Ithaca, NY: Cornell University Press, 2010.

Mahler, Anne Garland. "The Writer as Superhero: Fighting the Colonial Curse in Junot Diaz's *The Brief Wondrous Life of Oscar Wao*." *Journal of Latin American Cultural Studies* 19, no. 2 (2010): 119–40.

Ibarrola-Armendáriz, Aitor. "Puerto Rican and Dominican Self-Portraits and Their Frames: The 'Autobiographical' Fiction of Esmeralda Santiago, Junot Díaz, and Julia Alvarez." In *Selves in Dialogue: A Transethnic Approach to American Life Writing*, edited by Begoña Simal, 181–205. Amsterdam, Netherlands: Rodopi, 2011.

Miller, Matthew L. "Trauma in Junot Diaz's *Drown*." *Notes on Contemporary Literature* 41, no. 1 (2011).

Miller, T. S. "Preternatural Narration and the Lens of Genre Fiction in Junot Diaz's *The Brief Wondrous Life of Oscar Wao*." *Science Fiction Studies* 38, no. 1 (2011): 92–114.

Patteson, Richard. "Textual Territory and Narrative Power in Junot Díaz's *The Brief Wondrous Life of Oscar Wao*." *Ariel* 42, no. 3–4 (2011): 5–20.

Railton, Ben. "Novelist-Narrators of the American Dream: The (Meta-)Realistic Chronicles of Cather, Fitzgerald, Roth, and Díaz." *American Literary Realism* 43, no. 2 (2011): 133–53.

Sáez, Elena Machado. "Dictating Desire, Dictating Diaspora: Junot Diaz's *The*

Brief Wondrous Life of Oscar Wao as Foundational Romance." *Contemporary Literature* 52, no. 3 (2011): 522–55.

Saldívar, José David. "Conjectures on 'Americanity' and Junot Díaz's 'Fukú Americanus' in *The Brief Wondrous Life of Oscar Wao*." *Global South* 5, no. 1 (2011): 120–36.

Saldívar, Ramón. "Historical Fantasy, Speculative Realism, and Postrace Aesthetics in Contemporary American Fiction." *American Literary History* 23, no. 3 (2011): 574–99.

O'Brien, Sean P. "Some Assembly Required: Intertextuality, Marginalization, and *The Brief Wondrous Life of Oscar Wao*." *Journal of the Midwest Modern Language Association* 45, no. 1 (2012): 75–94.

Kondali, Ksenija. "Living in Two Languages: The Challenges to English in Contemporary American Literature." *ELOPE: English Language Overseas Perspectives and Enquires* 9 (2012): 101–13.

Mermann-Jozwiak, Elisabeth Maria. "Beyond Multiculturalism: Ethnic Studies, Transnationalism, and Junot Diaz's *Oscar Wao*." *ARIEL: A Review of International English Literature* 43, no. 2 (2012): 1–24.

Rader, Pamela. "'Trawling in Silences': Finding Humanity in the Páginas en Blanco of History in Junot Díaz's *The Brief Wondrous Life of Oscar Wao*." *Label Me Latina/o* 2 (Spring 2012): n.p. http://labelmelatin.com/wp-content /uploads/2012/02/%E2%80%9CTrawling-in-Silences%E2%80%9D-Finding-Humanity-in-the-P%C3%A1ginas-en-Blanco-of-History-in-Junot-D%C3%ADaz%E2%80%99s-The-Brief-Wondrous-Life-of-Oscar-Wao.pdf.

Saldívar, José David. *Trans-Americanity: Subaltern Modernities, Global Coloniality, and the Cultures of Greater Mexico*. Durham, NC: Duke University Press, 2012.

Balée, Susan. "Caves, Masks, and Code Switching: The Inventive Narratives of Junot Díaz." *Hudson Review* 66, no. 2 (2013): 337–52.

Casielles-Suárez, Eugenia. "Radical Code-Switching in *The Brief Wondrous Life of Oscar Wao*." *Bulletin of Hispanic Studies* 90, no. 4 (2013): 475–87.

Del Pilar Blanco, María. "Reading the Novum World: The Literary Geography of Science Fiction in Junot Díaz's *The Brief Wondrous Life of Oscar Wao*." In *Surveying the American Tropics: A Literary Geography from New York to Rio*, edited by Maria Cristina Fumagalli, Peter Hulme, Owen Robinson, and Lesley Wylie, 49–74. Liverpool: Liverpool University Press, 2013.

Figueroa, Víctor. "Disseminating 'El Chivo': Junot Díaz's Response to Mario Vargas Llosa in *The Brief Wondrous Life of Oscar Wao*." *Chasqui* 42, no. 1 (2013): 95–108.

Garden, Rebecca. "Distance Learning: Empathy and Culture in Junot Díaz's 'Wildwood.'" *Journal of Medical Humanities* 34, no. 4 (2013): 439–50.

Gasztold, Brygida. "A Dominican-American Experience of Not Quite Successful Assimilation: Junot Díaz's *The Brief Wondrous Life of Oscar Wao*." In *Crossroads in Literature and Culture*, edited by Jacek Fabiszak, Ewa Urbaniak-Rybicka, and Bartosz Wolski, 209–22. Berlin: Springer, 2013.

Kunsa, Ashley. "History, Hair, and Reimagining Racial Categories in Junot Díaz's *The Brief Wondrous Life of Oscar Wao*." *Critique: Studies in Contemporary Fiction* 54, no. 2 (2013): 211–24.

LaFargue, Ferentz. "Identity and Popular Culture in Toni Morrison's *The Bluest Eye* and Junot Díaz's *The Brief Wondrous Life of Oscar Wao*." In *Cultural Encounters*, edited by Nicholas Birns, 69–88. Ipswich, MA: Salem Press, 2013.

Lanzendörfer, Tim. "The Marvelous History of the Dominican Republic in Junot Díaz's *The Brief Wondrous Life of Oscar Wao*." *MELUS* 38, no. 2 (2013): 127–42.

Lopez-Calvo, Ignacio. "Junot Díaz." In *The Contemporary Spanish-American Novel: Bolaño and After*, edited by Will H. Corral, Nicholas Birns, and Juan E. De Castro, 406–10. New York: Bloomsbury, 2013.

Manzanas Calvo, Ana María. "Junot Díaz's 'Otravida, Otravez' and *Hospitalia*: The Workings of Hostile Hospitality." *Journal of Modern Literature* 37, no. 1 (2013): 107–23.

Perez, Richard. "Flashes of Transgression: The Fukú, Negative Aesthetics, and the Future in *The Brief Wondrous Life of Oscar Wao* by Junot Díaz." In *Moments of Magical Realism in U.S. Ethnic Literatures*, edited by Lyn Di Iorio Sandín and Richard Perez, 91–108. New York: Palgrave Macmillan, 2013.

Ramírez, Dixa. "Great Men's Magic: Charting Hyper-Masculinity and Supernatural Discourses of Power in Junot Díaz's *The Brief Wondrous Life of Oscar Wao*." *Atlantic Studies* 10, no. 3 (2013): 384–405.

Stringer, Dorothy. "Passing and the State in Junot Díaz's 'Drown.'" *MELUS* 38, no. 2 (2013): 111–26.

Graulund, Rune. "Generous Exclusion: Register and Readership in Junot Díaz's *The Brief Wondrous Life of Oscar Wao*." *MELUS* 39, no. 3 (2014): 31–48.

Hoberek, Andrew. *Considering Watchmen: Poetics, Property, Politics*. New Brunswick, NJ: Rutgers University Press, 2014.

Horn, Maja. *Masculinity after Trujillo: The Politics of Gender in Dominican Literature*. Gainesville: University of Florida Press, 2014.

Nadal, Marita, and Mónica Calvo. *Trauma in Contemporary Literature: Narrative and Representation*. New York: Routledge, 2014.

Orlando, Valérie, and Sandra M. Cypess. *Reimagining the Caribbean: Conversations*

Among the Creole, English, French, and Spanish Caribbean. Lanham, MD: Lexington, 2014.

Vargas, Jennifer Harford. "Dictating a Zafa: The Power of Narrative Form in Junot Díaz's *The Brief Wondrous Life of Oscar Wao.*" *MELUS* 39, no. 3 (2014): 8–30.

Weese, Katherine. "'Tú no Eres Nada de Dominicano': Unnatural Narration and De-Naturalizing Gender Constructs in Junot Díaz's *The Brief Wondrous Life of Oscar Wao.*" *Journal of Men's Studies* 22, no. 2 (2014): 89–104.

Pifano, Diana. "Reinterpreting the Diaspora and the Political Violence of the Trujillo Regime: The Fantastic as a Tool for Cultural Mediation in *The Brief Wondrous Life of Oscar Wao.*" *Belphégor* 12, no. 1 (2014): n.p. http://belphegor. revues.org/454.

INTERVIEWS

"Fiction Is the Poor Man's Cinema: An Interview with Junot Díaz." By Diogenes Cespedes and Silvio Torres-Saillant. *Callaloo* 23, no. 3 (2000): 892–907.

"Driven: Junot Díaz." In *Conversations with Ilan Stavans*, edited by Ilan Stavans, 47–51. Tucson: University of Arizona Press, 2005.

"'Wondrous Life' Explores Multinationality." By Terry Gross. *Fresh Air*. NPR, October 18, 2007. http://www.npr.org/templates/story/story.php?storyId =15400391.

"LAist Interview: Junot Diaz, Author and Pulitzer Prize Winner." By Carrie Meathrell and Osmany Rodriguez. *LAist*, April 10, 2008. http://laist.com/ 2008/04/10/laist_interview_134.php.

"Junot Díaz." By Edwidge Danticat. *BOMB* 101 (Fall 2007): 89–95.

"Junot Díaz." By Juleyka Lantigua. *The Progressive*, September 2007, 33–36.

"Conversation with Junot Díaz (To the Woman in the Mountain Cabin)." By Albert Jordy Raboteau. *Callaloo* 31, no. 3 (2008): 919–22.

"I'm Nobody or I'm a Nation." By Jesse Ellison. *Newsweek*, April 3, 2008. http:// www.newsweek.com/id/130350.

"In Conversation: Richard Price and Junot Díaz." *New York*, October 6, 2008: 130–32, 134.

"Author Junot Diaz Shares Thanksgiving Memories." By Steve Inskeep. *Morning Edition*. NPR, November 27, 2008. http://www.npr.org/templates/story/ story.php?storyId=97568937.

"In Darkness We Meet: A Conversation with Junot Díaz." By David Shook and Armando Celayo. *World Literature Today* 82, no. 2 (2008): 12–17.

"*Mil Máscaras*: An Interview with Pulitzer-Winner Junot Díaz (*The Brief Wondrous Life of Oscar Wao*)." By Matt Okie. *Identitytheory.com*, September 2, 2008. http://www.identitytheory.com/interviews/okie_diaz.php.

"A Conversation with Junot Díaz." By Achy Obejas. *Review: Literature and Arts of the Americas*, 42, no. 1 (2009): 42–47.

"The Science of Creativity." By Paul Dempsey. *Engineering & Technology* 4, no. 19 (2009): 78–79.

"Junot Díaz: The New Fiction Hero." By Rachel Chambers. *Art Culture: Contemporary Art, Innovation and Design*, February 27, 2009. http://www.artculture.com/culture/books-and-authors/junot-diaz-the-new-fiction-hero.

"Nerdsmith." By Adriana Lopez. *Guernicamag.com*, July 7, 2009. http://www.guernicamag.com/interviews/nerdsmith/.

"Small Talk: Junot Diaz." By Anna Metcalf. *Financial Times*, February 14, 2009, 17.

"Words on a Page: An Interview with Junot Díaz." By Anna Barnet. *Theharvardadvocate.com*, Spring 2009. http://www.theharvardadvocate.com/content/words-page-interview-junot-diaz?page=show.

"How I Write." By Sarah Anne Johnson. *Writer*, December 2010, 58.

"'The important things hide in plain sight': A Conversation with Junot Díaz." By Marisel Moreno. *Latino Studies* 8, no. 4 (2010): 532–42.

"Junot Díaz." In *Unpacking My Library: Writers and Their Books*, by Leah Price, 42–59. New Haven, CT: Yale University Press, 2011.

"Conversation: Junot Díaz." By Jeffrey Brown. *PBS Newshour*. PBS, September 28, 2012. http://www.pbs.org/newshour/art/junot-diaz/.

Harvest of Empire: The Untold Story of Latinos in America. Directed by Peter Getzels and Eduardo Lopez. Tampa, FL: Onyx Media Group, 2012. DVD.

"Growing the Hell Up: From Middle Earth to NJ." By Richard Wolinsky. *Guernicamag.com*, November 1, 2012. http://www.guernicamag.com/interviews/growing-the-hell-up-from-middle-earth-to-nj/.

"Junot Díaz Talks Dying Art, the Line Between Fact and Fiction, and What Scares Him Most." By Ross Scarano. *Complex.com*, December 17, 2012. http://www.complex.com/pop-culture/2012/12/junot-diaz-interview.

"'We exist in a constant state of translation. We just don't like it.'" By Karen Cresci. Buenosairesreview.org, May 4, 2013. http://www.buenosairesreview.org/2013/05/diaz-constant-state-of-translation/.

"Interview: Junot Díaz." By Hector Luis Alamo. Gozamos.com, November 21, 2013. http://gozamos.com/2013/11/interview-junot-diaz/.

ADDITIONAL CITED AND CONSULTED WORKS

Rabinowitz, Peter J. *Before Reading: Narrative Conventions and the Politics of Interpretation*. Columbus: Ohio State University Press, 1987.

Tolkien, J. R. R. *The Lord of the Rings*. Boston: Houghton Mifflin, 1994. First published 1954–55 by Allen & Unwin.

Torres-Saillant, Silvio. "The Tribulations of Blackness: Stages in Dominican Racial Identity." *Callaloo* 23, no. 3 (2000): 1086–111.

Stavans, Ilan. *Spanglish: The Making of a New American Language*. New York: Rayo, 2003.

Andrews, George Reid. *Afro-Latin America*. New York: Oxford University Press, 2004.

Nericcio, William Anthony. *Tex[t] Mex: Seductive Hallucinations of the "Mexican" in America*. Austin: University of Texas Press, 2007.

Tolkien, J. R. R. "On Fairy Stories." In *Tolkien on Fairy-Stories*, edited by Verlyn Flieger and Douglas A. Anderson, 42–59. New York: HarperCollins, 2008.

Cisneros, Sandra. *The Leonard Lopate Show*. 93.9 WNYC. April 23, 2009.

Olliz Boyd, Antonio. *The Latin American Identity and the African Diaspora: Ethnogenesis in Context*. Amherst, NY: Cambria Press, 2010.

Johnson, Susan. "*Harry Potter*, Eucatastrophe, and Christian Hope." *Logos* 14, no. 1: (2011).

Hatfield, Charles. *Hand of Fire: The Comics Art of Jack Kirby*. Jackson: University Press of Mississippi, 2012.

Hirsch, Edward. *A Poet's Glossary*. New York: Houghton Mifflin Harcourt, 2014.

INDEX